S0-BNT-547

SETTING YOU FREE TO MAKE
RIGHT CHOICES

JR. HIGH/SR. HIGH EDITION

JOSH MCDOWELL

World Bridge Press
Nashville, Tennessee

© Copyright 1995 by World Bridge Press
All rights reserved

Reprinted July 1995, September 1995, March 1996,
May 1997, December 1998

Item 7800-08
ISBN 0-8054-9828-1

Distributed to the trade by Broadman and Holman Publishers.

Dewey Decimal Classification: 248.83
Subject Heading: DECISION MAKING/CHOICE (PSYCHOLOGY)/YOUTH—RELIGIOUS

Unless otherwise indicated, biblical quotations are from: The Holy Bible, *New International Version*, copyright © 1973, 1978, 1984 by International Bible Society. Used by permission.

Verses marked KJV are taken from the *King James Version* of the Bible.

Verses marked NASB are from the *New American Standard Bible*.
Copyright © The Lockman Foundation, 1960, 1962, 1963, 1971, 1972, 1973, 1975, 1977. Used by permission.

Printed in the United States of America

World Bridge Press
127 Ninth Avenue, North
Nashville, Tennessee 37234

table of contents

Acknowledgment

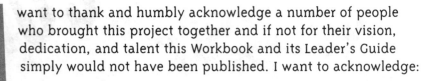

want to thank and humbly acknowledge a number of people who brought this project together and if not for their vision, dedication, and talent this Workbook and its Leader's Guide simply would not have been published. I want to acknowledge:

Jimmy Draper, Gene Mims, and Chuck Wilson with the Baptist Sunday School Board and Broadman and Holman for their vision and commitment to the Right from Wrong message and campaign.

John Kramp for his skilled leadership, publishing vision for the *Right from Wrong* Workbooks, and his untiring efforts as he championed this project on behalf of the publisher.

Dave Bellis, my associate of 18 years, for directing every aspect of the Right from Wrong Campaign and as managing writer of this project for developing and focusing the content and developing each product within the campaign into a coordinated campaign package.

Bob Hostetler who coauthored the *Right from Wrong* book with me for his spiritual insights, unselfish dedication, and incredible writing skills as he translated the Right from Wrong message so effectively to a junior high and senior high student mind-set.

Paul Turner, Barbara Hammond, and Kathy Edwards for their insights, educational design skills, and editing expertise as they readied the manuscript for publication.

Josh McDowell

How to Use This Book

Some books are like riding in a plane; you sit down, fasten your seat belt, and the pilot flies you to your destination. Other books are like driving a race car; you're doing the driving, but you know the track has already been laid out for you. The *Right Choices Student Workbook* is more like steering a dirt bike across the surface of the moon; you're not sure what you'll find, but it's bound to be a wild ride!

This Workbook is designed to lead you on a wild ride of discovery. You'll find out many things you did not know—things about yourself, things about the people around you, things about truth, things about God. You may discover some unexpected things, too, but one thing's for sure: it's bound to be a wild ride.

The *Right Choices Student Workbook* is not designed to be read like a novel. It is intended to guide you through a daily process of discovery toward developing a habit of making right choices, choices that will bring you the best rewards and the greatest satisfaction.

To get the most out of this Workbook, set aside a specific time every day to study each day's assignment (one assignment will usually take less than 15 minutes). Take your time; don't try to jump ahead, or complete several days' assignments in one sitting. Also, don't skip any assignments; each day builds on the previous day's discovery and leads to the next, so skipping over a day or two will rob you of crucial understanding and insight.

These studies are also designed to be used in connection with weekly group meetings, that will help clarify or amplify your understanding of the concepts you learn in the Workbook. Be as faithful as possible to the group sessions, and you will reap even greater rewards from your personal study.

You are on the verge of learning a process that could very well change your life. Buckle your seat belt. Fasten your helmet. A dirt bike ride on the moon can be a jarring experience.

week 1

week

week

one

The Club

magine being approached by a friend at school.

"Hey," your friend says, "have you heard about 'the club'?"

"You mean that thing people put on their steering wheels so no one can steal their car?"

"No, I mean the new club, the new organization everyone's talking about." "I haven't heard a thing," you answer.

"Where have you been? It's the best! Look, I've got a membership card all filled out for you."

"Wait a minute," you say. "What do I get for joining?"

"Well, for one, just by joining you can double your tendency to get drunk or steal, and triple your chances of getting involved in illegal drug use!"

"Why would I want to do that?" you ask, but your friend seems not to hear.

"You'll become two times more likely to feel disappointed and resentful, two times more likely to lack purpose, and six times more likely to attempt suicide!"

Would you join a club like that? No? Well, believe it or not, you may already be a member of a club that makes you:

- 36% more likely to lie to a parent or other adult
- 48% more likely to cheat on an exam
- 2 times more likely to try to physically hurt someone
- 2 times more likely to watch a pornographic film
- 2 1/4 times more likely to steal
- 3 times more likely to use illegal drugs
- 6 times more likely to attempt suicide

Membership in "the club" will not only affect your behavior, however; it will also affect your attitudes, making you:

- 65% more likely to mistrust people
- 2 times more likely to be disappointed
- 2 times more likely to be angry with life
- 2 times more likely to be resentful

The five daily sessions that follow this brief introduction are designed to help you determine whether you have unknowingly joined "the club" and to provide instruction on how to cancel your membership.

Are You a Member?

d ay 1

How can a person join a club without knowing it? Have you ever confided in a friend about, say, your frustration in trying to understand someone of the opposite sex, only to hear your friend say, "Join the club"?

Have you complained about how you wish your geometry teacher would—just once—forget to assign homework for the weekend, only to hear your friend say, "Join the club"?

Have you confessed your struggles to get the attention of that gorgeous new exchange student from Sweden, only to hear your friend say, "Join the club"?

Maybe your friend never says that, but you can see how it is possible to unknowingly be part of a larger group, even when you thought you were alone. Sometimes that's good. Other times, of course, it's bad.

How can you find out, however, if you're a member of the club we spoke about in the introduction? How can you discover if you're in that vulnerable category we talked about, in which your tendency to get drunk is doubled, your chances of getting involved in illegal drug use are tripled, and your tendency to attempt suicide is increased sixfold? How can you determine whether you're more likely to feel disappointed and resentful than, say Eugene Dimwicz, the kid who sits next to you in homeroom?

The Entrance Exam

One way to determine whether you are a member of "the club" is to take the Entrance Exam. Don't panic—it's a short, simple quiz consisting of seven "opinion" questions. It shouldn't take you more than a few moments to complete it.

First, clear your desk of all books and papers. . . just kidding. Simply mark one answer next to each statement to indicate whether you agree or disagree with that statement.

This Week's Verse—

"You will know the truth, and the truth will set you free."
John 8:32

	Yes	No	Not Sure

Statement

1. There is no such thing as "absolute truth"; people may define truth in contradictory ways and still be correct. ___ ___ ___

2. Everything in life is negotiable. ___ ___ ___

3. Only the Bible provides a clear and indisputable description of moral truth. ___ ___ ___

4. Nothing can be known for certain except the things you experience in your life. ___ ___ ___

5. When it comes to matters of morals and ethics, truth means different things to different people; no one can be sure they have the truth. ___ ___ ___

6. What is right for one person in a given situation might not be right for another person who encounters that same situation. ___ ___ ___

7. God may know the meaning of truth, but humans are not capable of grasping that knowledge. ___ ___ ___

Scoring Yourself

Now, how do you grade yourself? It's simple. Circle the point value below that corresponds to each of your answers to the Entrance Exam on page 9:

Question	Yes	No	Not Sure
1.	0	1	0
2.	0	1	0
3.	1	0	0
4.	0	1	0
5.	0	1	0
6.	0	1	0
7.	0	1	0

If your score totals 7 points, you're not a member of "the club."

If your score totals 5-6 points, you're a bronze member of "the club"; you stand a good chance of effectively canceling your membership.

If your score totals 3-4 points, you're a silver member; your membership can be revoked with a little thought, and a little work.

If your score totals 1-2 points, you're a gold member of "the club." Apply yourself diligently to this study, and you'll be out of "the club" in no time.

If your score totals 0 points, you must be a charter member of "the club"! Hold on tight; you've got a wild ride of exciting new discoveries ahead of you.

How do you react to the Entrance Exam? _____

Do you disagree with the conclusions of the exam?

❏ Yes ❏ No

Why or why not? _____

_____

How does your score on the exam make you feel?

❏ Disappointed   ❏ Happy
❏ Scared   ❏ Worried
❏ Unconcerned   ❏ Upset
❏ Angry   ❏ Confused
❏ Satisfied   ❏ _____

What Do You Know?

Each of the questions in the Entrance Exam on page 9 reveals what you believe about absolute truth. Only one of the questions uses that phrase, but all of them measure whether or not you believe truth is absolute. . . or relative.

You see, some people believe in absolute truth; that is, they believe that there are some things that are true for all people, for all times, and for all places. Others, of course, don't accept an absolute standard of truth; they believe that all truth is relative, that the line between right and wrong is different for everyone. They believe that people may define *truth* in contradictory ways and still be correct, that truth means different things to different people, that what is right for one person in a given situation might not be right for another person in that same situation.

Jesus, of course, revealed what He believed about truth when He said,

"You will know the truth, and the truth will set you free"
(John 8:32).

How do you find yourself responding to the Entrance Exam and to Jesus' words? (check one)

❏ I don't believe in absolute truth.
❏ I believe in absolute truth.
❏ I believe in absolute truth, but I don't know what the truth is.
❏ I guess I'm not sure what I believe.
❏ other_____.

Reviewing Your Membership

• Take a few moments to review today's lesson. Did you discover anything new?

❏ Yes   ❏ No

If so, what was it?_____

_____

_____

• Based on what you've learned today, how would you define *absolute truth?*

_____

_____

_____

Absolute truth = that which is true for all people, for all times, and for all places.

• Do you think what you believe about absolute truth affects your attitudes or behavior?

❏ Yes   ❏ No

Why or why not? _____

_____

_____

_____

• If you could cancel your membership in "the club" right now, would you do it?

❏ Yes   ❏ No

Why or why not? _____

_____

_____

_____

Canceling Your Membership

You dial the number: "1-800-The Club."

A soothing voice answers after three rings. "Thank you for calling The Club. This is Pat."

"Uh, yeah," you say. "I want to cancel my membership."

"Is there a problem with your membership?"

"Well, yeah," you say.

"Do you realize that canceling your membership would revoke all your benefits?"

"Well, yeah," you answer slowly. "What benefits?"

"And you'll miss out on our special?"

"Special?"

"Yes. Two months free membership."

"I don't pay anything now," you say.

"Well, this way you get an extra two months at no cost!"

"But. . ."

"And," the voice on the line adds grandly, "I'll enter you into our drawing!"

"Drawing?" you echo.

"Absolutely." You hear the sound of clacking computer keys on the other end. "A drawing for a lifetime membership for you and a friend! You can give it as a gift!"

"But I just wanted to. . ."

"I'll just need your name and address for the computer, okay?"

"But I. . ."

"Please give me your last name first and your first name last, followed by your street number and street name, city, state, zip code, and maternal grandmother's maiden name."

"But. . ."

"Is that your last name or your first name?"

Is it really so tough to cancel your membership in "the club"? No. There's no 800 number, and no "club headquarters" to call, but membership can be canceled, nonetheless.

Finding the Solution

To find out how to cancel your membership in "the club," fill in the blanks in the activity at the top of page 13 with words that correspond to the given meaning. Then transfer each letter to the numbered space in the answer. When you are finished, the answer will reveal how to cancel your membership in "the club."

A tooth doctor

— — — — — — —
34 14 24 5 33 12 22

An emergency sound

— — — — —
40 4 27 8 15

To repair something

— — —
19 11 10

Not alive

— — — —
2 41 26 25

Fine particles of dirt

— — — —
28 38 32 6

A baked lump of bread

— — — —
42 18 1 43

It pumps blood

— — — — —
7 17 23 39 31

A wild dog-like animal

— — — — — —
16 29 36 37 13 9

To entertain with humor

— — — — —
20 3 30 21 35

Cancel your membership in "the club" today.

ANSWER:
In order to cancel your membership in "the club," you must:

— — — — —   — — —   — — — — — — — — —
1 2 3 4 5   6 7 8   9 10 11 12 13 14 15 16 17

— —   —   — — — — — — —
18 19   20   21 22 23 24 25 26 27 28

— — — — — — —   — — — — — — — — .
29 30 31 32 33 34 35   36 37 38 39 40 41 42 43

What Does It Mean?

So that's how you cancel your membership in "the club"! But what does that mean?

Do you remember the quiz you took in the group session? Each question in that quiz pointed to a standard, something outside yourself or your own opinion that would provide the answer you sought: a dictionary, a rule book, a test key. Those things are standards, accepted authorities by which you can measure things.

Many of us refer to such standards repeatedly in our daily lives, but we resist doing so when it comes to decisions about right or wrong. Why do you think we do that?

_____

_____

_____

_____

_____

_____

A Garden Party

The Bible records a famous example of the human tendency to want to make moral decisions on our own, without referring to or submitting to any outside standard.

> Now the serpent was more crafty than any of the wild animals the Lord God had made. He said to woman, "Did God really say, 'You must not eat from any tree in the garden'?"
>
> The woman said to the serpent, "We may eat fruit from the trees in the garden, but God did say, 'You must not eat from the tree that is in the middle of the garden...'"
>
> "You will not surely die," the serpent said to the woman. "For God knows that when you eat of it your eyes will be opened, and you will be like God, knowing good and evil."
>
> When the woman saw that the fruit of the tree was good for food and pleasing to the eye. . . she took some and ate it (Gen. 3:1-6).

Do you think Eve's mistake was:

❏ eating the fruit
❏ wanting to make her own decision about what was right or wrong
❏ something else
❏ all the above

Eve was a member of the club we talked about earlier! Do you think she might have acted differently if she had admitted that the standard for what was right or wrong was not inside herself?

❏ Yes   ❏ No

How do you think Eve's story relates to you?_____

_____

_____

_____

Do you ever act like Eve?

❑ Yes   ❑ No

If so, how?_____

_____

_____

Do you find yourself wanting to accept or wanting to reject the point of today's study?

❑ Accept   ❑ Reject

Why do you think you're reacting the way you are?_____

_____

_____

_____

Why do you think you're reacting the way you are?

Based on your answer to the above question, compose a brief prayer below, explaining your feelings to God and asking Him to prepare you for tomorrow's study.

The Standard We Need—
Part One

day 3

Imagine trying to measure a baseball diamond without any idea how far from each other the bases should be. Imagine trying to write a story about macroglobulinemia without ever having heard of a dictionary, or trying to bake a cake without measuring any quantities. That's the problem faced by the members of "the club." They have no standard outside themselves by which to measure the rightness or wrongness of their actions. They are so often disappointed or angry with life because they tend to believe that no such standard exists. They think that they alone decide what is right or wrong in every circumstance.

But aren't they right? After all, what kind of standard is there for making decisions about right and wrong? You can't measure out a cup of "right." There is no "dictionary" of right and wrong deeds. Even if we're willing to admit the existence of a standard outside ourselves, where do we look?

Which of the following would you accept as a standard to define what is right or wrong? (check all that apply)

- ❑ Your favorite teacher
- ❑ Your parents
- ❑ A Sunday School lesson
- ❑ Public opinion
- ❑ The Bill of Rights
- ❑ Your conscience
- ❑ Your favorite song
- ❑ The Communist manifesto
- ❑ The government
- ❑ Your horoscope
- ❑ A Josh McDowell book
- ❑ Your best friend

Do you consider any of the above to be acceptable standards?

❑ Yes ❑ No

Why or why not? _____

_____

Have you been relying on any of the things on the list above? Have you trusted some of those things to define right and wrong for you?

❑ Yes ❑ No

If yes, what has been the result? _____

_____

What is it about the things on the list above that make them
unacceptable standards?_____

_____

_____

And remember, the lack of an acceptable standard that is outside yourself results in automatic membership in "the club." And membership in
"the club" can have some pretty disastrous consequences.

"I Confess—She Did It!"

Read *Genesis 3:1-13*, the story of Eve and Adam's enrollment into "the
club." When God confronted the two apple thieves about their terrible
choice, they each revealed the standards by which they were trying to
measure their actions.

To what standard did Adam compare himself *(v. 12)*? _____

To what standard did Eve compare herself *(v. 13)*? _____

Now read *Genesis 3:14-24*, and list below some of the consequences
Adam and Eve faced because of their membership in "the club."

_____

_____

_____

All choices have
consequences.

Adam and Eve's choice turned out so badly because neither of their
standards was an appropriate standard. Similarly, none of the standards in
the list on page 16 is what we need, because none of them possess all the
requirements for a true standard of right and wrong. Those qualities are
hidden in the word search on page 18. After you have found and circled all
the words in the list, the remaining letters will spell out the three qualities
a true standard of right and wrong must possess.

Find the following words:

right
wrong
relative
absolute
moral
immoral
good
evil
do
don't
truth
choice
bad
standard

```
R  I  G  H  T  O  E  B  J  E  D
C  T  N  E  V  I  T  A  L  E  R
I  V  O  E  T  R  U  T  H  C  A
U  N  R  L  N  I  L  V  E  I  D
R  S  W  A  O  A  O  E  L  O  N
D  C  O  R  D  N  S  V  S  H  A
A  D  O  O  G  T  B  I  A  C  T
B  I  M  M  O  R  A  L  N  T  S
```

The uncircled letters, in order, form the following three requirements of a true standard of right and wrong, which must be:

__ __ __ __ __ __ __ __,

__ __ __ __ __ __ __ __ __, and

__ __ __ __ __ __ __ __.

That is the kind of standard we need, and tomorrow's study will feature more explanation of why such a standard is necessary.

Close today's study by spending a few moments in prayer, asking God
• to help you understand any concepts you're finding difficult to grasp
• to help you apply yourself to this study
• to help you, by His Holy Spirit, to hear and obey the truth of His Word.

The Standard We Need – Part Two

You wake up the morning of your 16th birthday and stumble into the kitchen for breakfast. Your mom greets you with a kiss and a bright, "Happy 16th birthday." You mutter a few sleepy words of thanks and reach into the cabinet for a cereal bowl.

"There's something out in the driveway for you," your mom says.

You turn and look at her. She's smiling broadly. Your eyes widen and your sleepiness is gone.

You slam the bowl down on the counter and dash through the door in your bathrobe and bare feet. Mom follows behind, still smiling.

You stop a few feet from the driveway and stare. Your mom catches up with you, drapes an arm around your shoulders, and squeezes.

"It's not new," she says, nodding toward the car in the driveway, "but it has a tape deck that works, just like you wanted."

You look at your mom and then back at the car.

"Where are the wheels?" you ask. The car is resting on blocks.

"You wanted wheels, too?" she asks innocently.

You step carefully to the driver's side of the car and look in.

"There's no steering wheel!" you announce in a voice of disbelief.

"What do you think of the tape deck?" your mom asks. "Pretty nice, huh?"

You reach into the car and pop the hood. You walk to the front of the car and lift the hood into the air.

"Mom!" you bellow, as if she'd just asked you to wear one of her dresses to the prom. "There's no engine!"

"You didn't say you wanted all those things. You just said you'd like a tape deck."

You let the hood drop. You turn to face your mother.

"Mom." You're trying not to shout. "It has to have 'all those things.' If it doesn't, it's not a car. . . it's just a piece of junk!"

Standard Equipment

No one would realistically expect a car to work without tires, a steering wheel, and an engine. Those things are the most basic equipment; without them, it's not a car, it's a piece of junk.

It is pretty much the same with finding a standard to help decide issues of right and wrong. A true standard must possess some basic equipment, or it's no standard at all—just a piece of junk.

Any standard that tells you what's right or wrong must, first of all, be *objective*. What does *objective* mean? (circle one)

Absolute truth is objective.

Objective:

1. what lawyers say in a courtroom when they don't like something

2. existing independently of individual thought or opinion

3. an emotional feeling that something is right

4. what nurses give you with those really big needles

A true standard of right and wrong must be *objective*; that is, it must exist independently of what you (or any other person) thinks or feels. Otherwise, right and wrong could change from person-to-person: you may consider stealing to be wrong, but your neighbor may not. In the absence of an objective standard of right and wrong, you have no basis on which to inform your neighbor that he should not swipe your large-screen TV with wrap-around sound.

That's the reason, in the quiz on page 16, "your conscience" was not a wholly satisfying answer. Your conscience is not an objective standard of right and wrong, because it does not exist independently of you, your opinions, and your feelings.

The second piece of equipment that a true standard of right and wrong must possess is that it must be *universal*. What does *universal* mean? (circle one)

Universal:

1. endorsed by a major Hollywood movie studio

2. popular among faculty and students at institutions of higher learning

3. acceptable and/or pleasing to everyone

4. applying to all people

Absolute truth is objective and universal.

A true standard of right and wrong must be not only objective, but also universal; that is, it must apply to all people in all places. If it did not, right and wrong may change from culture-to-culture or even from community-to-community. You may consider it wrong to abuse children, for example, but if a neighboring culture disagrees, who can say they're wrong. In the absence of a universal standard of right and wrong, you have no basis on which to inform your neighbors that it is wrong to treat their children—or yours—in despicable ways.

That is why, in the quiz on page 16, "the government" or "public opinion" were not wholly satisfying answers. Those things are not universal standards, because they do not apply to all people.

The third piece of equipment that a true standard of right and wrong must possess is that it must be constant. What does that mean? (circle one)

Constant:

1. one of the twin Roman cities in what is now Turkey (the other was Inople)
2. does not change with time
3. the opposite of instant
4. a title of nobility, similar in rank to Duke and Earl

A true standard of right and wrong must be not only objective and universal, it must also be *constant*; that is, it must be unchanging. Otherwise, right and wrong might be different from generation-to-generation, or even from day-to-day. For example, you may consider racism to be wrong, but if standards of right and wrong can change over time, then you cannot condemn the atrocities of Nazi Germany nor the slavery of pre-Civil War America. In the absence of a constant standard of right and wrong, you have no hope of knowing, from one minute to the next, whether an act is right or wrong.

That is why, in the quiz on page 16, "the Bill of Rights" was not a wholly satisfying answer. Although it is a marvelous document, it is not the ultimate standard we need, because it can change from year-to-year. That is fine for a constitutional document, but it does not meet the requirement for a true standard of right and wrong.

Absolute truth is objective, universal, and constant.

Where the Rubber Meets the Road

When Solomon became king of Israel, he prayed,

> "Now, O Lord my God, you have made your servant king in place of my father David. But I am only a little child and do not know how to carry out my duties. . . . So give your servant a discerning heart to govern your people and to distinguish between right and wrong" (1 Kings 3:7,9).

Do you think Solomon's prayer affirms a belief in an objective, universal, and constant standard of right and wrong?

❑ Yes ❑ No

Why do you think Solomon would ask for the ability to distinguish between right and wrong?_____

_____

_____

What would that kind of ability do for you? _____

_____

_____

Spend a few moments thoughtfully completing the following statements:

An objective standard of right and wrong would help me to _____

_____

_____

A universal standard of right and wrong would help me to _____

_____

_____

A constant standard of right and wrong would help me to _____

_____

_____

Tomorrow's study will complete our search for the standard we need.

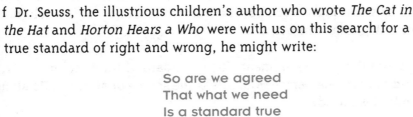

The Standard We Need – Part Three

If Dr. Seuss, the illustrious children's author who wrote *The Cat in the Hat* and *Horton Hears a Who* were with us on this search for a true standard of right and wrong, he might write:

> So are we agreed
> That what we need
> Is a standard true
> For me <u>and</u> you
> For all humankind
> And for all time
> For every race
> In every place?
> We may be agreed
> That that's our need,
> But what can fill
> Such a big bill?

Okay, so it's no *Green Eggs and Ham,* but the lines above do point out our problem. It's one thing to say that a true objective of right and wrong must be objective, universal, and constant, but where—realistically speaking—can we hope to find such a standard?

Look back at the list of choices on page 16. Do any of the choices meet all three requirements for a true standard of right and wrong? Are any of those potential "standards" objective, universal, *and* constant?

❏ Yes   ❏ No

If none of the choices on page 16 "fills the bill," as Dr. Seuss might have put it, where do we look? Where can we find a standard that is:
- outside ourselves
- above ourselves
- before and beyond ourselves?

God on the Stage

Back in the days of Julius Caesar, there was a Roman poet and satirist named Horace. Horace criticized the laziness of many playwrights of his day. He strongly criticized those writers who, every time a problem occurred in the plot of their play, brought in one of the many Roman gods to solve it. Horace instructed, Do not "let a god come in [on to the stage] unless the difficulty be worthy of such an intervention."[1]

The challenge of trying to distinguish right from wrong is one that deserves—in fact, demands—a God to solve it. It is impossible to arrive at an objective, universal, and constant standard of truth and morality without bringing God onto the stage. If an objective standard of truth and morality exists, it cannot be the product of the human mind (or it will not be objective); it must be the product of another Mind. If a universal rule of right and wrong exists, it must transcend individual experience (or it will not be universal); it must be above us all, something—or someone—that is common to all humanity, to all creation. If a constant and unchanging truth exists, it must reach beyond human time lines (or it would not be constant); it must be eternal.

Those things, requirements for a standard of truth and morality, are found only in one person—God. He is the source of all truth. He alone is the Standard we need.

He is objective (fill in the blanks in the verses below to understand God as the objective source of truth):

He is the Rock, his work is _____ . . .
a God of _____ and without
iniquity, _____ and _____
is he (Deut. 32:4, KJV).

As for God, his way is _____;
the word of the Lord is _____ . . . .
For who is God besides the Lord? And who
is the Rock except our God? (Ps. 18:30).

He is universal (fill in the blanks in the verses below to understand God as the universal source of truth):

The mountains melt like wax before the
Lord, before the Lord _____
_____
(Ps. 97:5).

For. . . the Holy One of Israel is your
Redeemer; he is called
_____
(Isa. 54:5).

The Lord has established his throne in
heaven, and his kingdom _____
_____
(Ps. 103:19).

He is constant (fill in the blanks in the verses below to understand God as the constant source of truth):

Do you not know? Have you not heard? The
Lord is _____ .
the Creator of the ends of the earth. He
will not grow tired or weary, and his
understanding no one can fathom (Isa. 40:28).

Everything God does _____
_____ ;
nothing can be added to it and nothing
taken from it (Eccl. 3:14).

You see, it is God's nature and character that defines truth. He defines what is right for all people, for all times, in all places. But truth is not something He decides; it is something He is.

The basis of everything we call moral, the source of every good thing, is the eternal God who is outside us, above us, and beyond us. The reason some things are right and some things are wrong is because there exists a Creator, Jehovah God, and He is a righteous God.

The reason we think that there are such things as "fair" and "unfair" is because our Maker is a just God.

The reason love is a virtue and hatred a vice is because the God who formed us is a God of love.

The reason honesty is right and deceit is wrong is because God is true.

The reason chastity is moral and promiscuity is immoral is because God is pure.

God is the standard we need.

How do you find yourself responding to today's study? _____

_____

_____

_____

Do you find it easy or difficult to accept God as the only true standard for right and wrong? (chart your response on the line below)

_____

easy   difficult

To what "standard" have you been comparing your behavior up until now?

❏ my own ideas of right and wrong
❏ my parents and what they say
❏ my friends and what they say
❏ my society and what it says
❏ my church and what it says
❏ other _____

Do you think this week's study will affect your actions and attitudes in the future?

❏ Yes   ❏ No

Truth is not something that God does, truth is what God is.

If so, in what way? _____

_____

_____

Spend a few moments in prayer, responding to what you have learned this week; close by speaking or singing the following biblical benediction:

Now to the King eternal, immortal, invisible, the only God be honor and glory for ever and ever. Amen (1 Tim. 1:17).

[1] J.K. Hoyt, *The Cyclopedia of Practical Quotations, Revised Edition* (New York & London: Funk & Wagnalls Co, 1896) 707.

week 2

Schindler and Sean

Some time ago, I took my 13-year-old daughter, my 17-year-old son, and his girlfriend to see Stephen Spielberg's movie, *Schindler's List*.

As we left the theater, we were surrounded by a somber crowd, many of whom were commenting on the atrocities inflicted upon the Jews by the Nazis. I turned to my son.

"Sean," I said, "do you believe the holocaust was wrong—morally wrong?"

He answered quickly. "Yes."

Then, as we got into the car to travel to a nearby town for dinner, I pursued the matter. "Almost everyone walking out of that theater would say the holocaust was wrong," I said. "But what basis would they have for making that judgment? Could they answer *why* it was wrong?"

I could see the wheels in three teenage minds spinning as I continued. "Most people in America subscribe to a view of morality called 'cultural ethics.' In other words, they believe that whatever is acceptable in that culture is moral; if the majority of people say a thing is 'right,' then it is right."

At about that time, we arrived at the restaurant and continued the discussion over dinner. "That's why many Americans will say that abortion is OK, because the majority of Americans—and Congress and the Supreme Court—have accepted it. If the majority thinks it's OK, it must be OK, right?

"But there's a problem with that," I explained. "If that is true, then how can we say the 'aborting' of six million Jews in the holocaust was wrong? In fact, the Nazis offered that very argument as a defense at the Nuremberg Trials. They argued, 'How can you come from another culture and condemn what we did when our culture said it was acceptable?' In condemning them, the world court said that there is something beyond culture, above culture, that determines right and wrong."

I also went on to explain that most of what people call morality today is simply pragmatism. "If we don't condemn what the Nazis did," people reason within themselves, "what's to stop someone from doing it to us?" And they're right, of course; they recognize the need for objective morality, but they cannot arrive at a true moral code—because they refuse to acknowledge the original.

Finally, after about two hours at the restaurant, I asked, "Do you know why what you saw tonight was wrong?"

"I know it was wrong," Sean ventured, "but I don't know why."

"There is a truth," I said, "that is outside me, above our family, and beyond any human—a truth about killing that originates in God. Killing is wrong because there is a God and that God is a living God, who created life and said, 'It is good,' and commanded us to preserve life and not to kill." In that conversation, I identified three keys to making right choices, three parts of a process that will help you make right choices. It is that process we will be discovering the next few days.

The Truth Process —Part One

Parents often say the strangest things. You may often be baffled and surprised by things your mother or father say. How many of the following phrases have you heard from your parents' mouths?

- ❏ "If you keep crossing your eyes, they're going to stick like that!"
- ❏ "Don't look at me in that tone of voice!"
- ❏ "Don't listen to what I say, listen to what I mean."
- ❏ "This is going to hurt me more than it'll hurt you."
- ❏ "Do you think I enjoy cleaning up after you"?
- ❏ "Children are starving in India, and you can't even finish your brussels sprouts!"
- ❏ "Do you want me to give you something to cry about"?
- ❏ "When I was your age . . ."
- ❏ "If I've told you once, I've told you a thousand times. . ."
- ❏ "Money doesn't grow on trees."

Some of those words sound familiar, don't they? It seems like every parent in the world has said those things at one time or another. You may not remember, but there are other phrases your parents have probably said repeatedly to you. See how many you can complete:

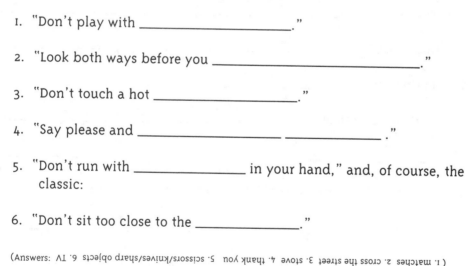

1. "Don't play with _____."

2. "Look both ways before you _____."

3. "Don't touch a hot _____."

4. "Say please and _____ _____ ."

5. "Don't run with _____ in your hand," and, of course, the classic:

6. "Don't sit too close to the _____."

(Answers: 1. matches 2. cross the street 3. stove 4. thank you 5. scissors/knives/sharp objects 6. TV)

Each of those phrases is a precept. When you were a child, much of the communication between you and your parents was in the form of precept. They repeatedly told you "do this," and "don't do that."

The Precepts of the Lord

Similarly, God has issued precepts—we usually call them commands—to His people. He has told us, "do this," and "don't do that" in language as clear as your mom saying, "look both ways before you cross the street."

This Week's Verse—

The law of the Lord is perfect, reviving the soul. The statutes of the Lord are trustworthy, making wise the simple.
Psalm 19:7

Look up the verses below in your Bible and complete each precept:

"You shall _____" (Ex. 20:3).
"Do not _____" (Matt. 7:1).
"Do not _____. Do not _____. Do not _____" (Lev. 19:11).
Avoid _____ (1 Thess. 4:3).
"You shall not _____" (Deut. 5:17).
"Love _____" (John 13:34).
Obey _____ and _____(Heb. 13:17).

The precepts above are just a few of the commands God gives in His Word. (Jewish tradition maintains that God gave 613 specific commands!)
God has communicated a lot about Himself to us through precept. His commands reveal what He likes, what He doesn't like, what He considers important, what He thinks is good, and what He thinks is bad. But the precepts of the Lord are not just a bunch of do's and don'ts, shalts and shalt–nots; they are designed also to lead us beyond the precept to the next step in the process of truth.

Reflexes and Responses

Complete the following sentences to express your response to today's study.

I'm feeling _____

I'm thinking _____

I'm having trouble _____

I'm starting to realize _____

_____

God is speaking to me through His Word, and He's saying _____

_____

Take a few moments to respond in prayer to what God's Word is teaching you.

Lord, Your Word is showing me
_____, and I want to respond by
_____. Please help me to
_____, and teach me Your ways, so that I
may know You and find favor with You. Amen.

REMEMBER THAT PRECEPTS ARE JUST THE FIRST STEP.

The Truth Process
—Part Two

"Y ou lied to me!" Amanda's mom said. She faced her daughter in the kitchen, a fist propped on each hip.

Amanda rolled her eyes. Her mother just didn't understand sometimes.

Her mom continued. "How could you lie to your own mother?"

"I had to, Mother," Amanda answered patiently. "You would never have let me go to the party if I'd told you it was at Steve Hanson's house." Her mom could be so unrealistic sometimes.

"You're right there, little lady."

Amanda hated it when her mother called her "little lady." She would turn 16 in two weeks, and her mother still treated her like a child. "Why are you making such a big deal out of this?" Amanda asked. "Nothing happened."

"I'm making a big deal out of it because it's wrong!"

"What was so wrong? I went to a fun party and you had a relaxing evening at home, without worrying about your 'little lady.'"

"What was so wrong? We've taught you better than that. Lying is wrong, Amanda Lynn."

Now she was pulling the middle name stuff. Amanda hated her middle name; she thought it made her sound like a musical instrument, "a mandolin."

"Why is it so wrong?" Amanda asked.

"Because it is," her mom answered.

"Oh, that's just great, Mother."

"Because the Bible says it's wrong," her mom countered.

"I told you, Mother. . ." Amanda began.

"'Thou shalt not lie.' Sound familiar?" her mom replied.

"I *had* to say what I said, okay?" Amanda retorted.

"'Honor your father and your mother.' Sound familiar?" her mother questioned then continued, "Why can't you just understand that?"

There's a lot going on in that conversation. We can learn a lot about Amanda and her mother just from that one conversation. But the thing that's most apparent is that Amanda's mom hasn't progressed beyond precept in her understanding of right and wrong. She has a point, of course—according to the Bible, according to the precepts of the Lord, lying is wrong. But the precepts also point to something else, something further that we can know about right and wrong.

The Principles of Right and Wrong

If all of God's commands are the first step toward knowing Him and distinguishing right from wrong, principles are the next step on the stairway, because behind each precept is a principle.

Principle = a rule or standard that may be applied to more than one type of situation.

A *principle* is "a rule or standard that may be applied to more than one type of situation." For example, your mom's precept to "say please and thank you" at the dinner table only applies to mealtimes. Her rule about writing a thank-you note (even to your grandmother for the flannel pajamas she buys you every Christmas) only applies when you've been given gifts. She insists that you cover your mouth when you cough or sneeze, but not when you're speaking to someone. All these different precepts apply to specific situations, but the comprehensive principle behind each specific precept is courtesy or politeness. The precept is specific; the principle is general.

Principles help explain the "why" behind a command. A concern for safety is one of the principles behind a mother's command to look both ways before crossing the street. Reverence for life is the principle behind the command, "Thou shalt not kill." A principle behind the command, "You shall not give false testimony," is honesty.

Learning to identify the principles behind God's precepts will help us see the overarching truth that applies, even when a specific command doesn't seem to apply.

Precepts and Principles

What is the principle, the "why," behind God's command to *avoid sexual immorality (1 Thess. 4:3)?* What is the principle, the overarching truth, behind God's command, *"Do not defraud your neighbor or rob him" (Lev. 19:13)?*

See if you can match the precepts with the principles they express (the first one has been done for you):

Principles help explain the "why" behind a precept.

Precept	Principle
Exodus 20:15	Purity
Exodus 23:6	Respect
Matthew 5:42	Honesty
Ephesians 6:1	Mercy
1 John 3:11	Self-Control
Isaiah 58:7	Unity
Ephesians 5:4	Justice
1 Corinthians 6:18	Love
Genesis 2:24	Generosity

Review and Response

• Have you discovered anything new as a result of this week's study?

❑ Yes ❑ No

If yes, what? _____

_____

_____

• Have you disobeyed any of the above precepts today? This week?

❑ Yes ❑ No

If yes, what? _____

_____

_____

• Has your life displayed any of the above principles today? This week?

❑ Yes ❑ No

If yes, what?_____

_____

_____

_____

• Do you react differently to the precepts than you do to the principles?

❑ Yes ❑ No

If yes, in what way?_____

_____

_____

_____

If yes, why do you think that is?_____

_____

_____

_____

_____

• What do you wish to say to God in response to today's study? Write your response below.

_____

_____

_____

_____

_____

_____

_____

_____

The Truth Process —Part Three

Knowing God's precepts (and even the principles of truth that lie behind those precepts) is not the end of the story. The process of discerning truth—of distinguishing right from wrong—leads from precept, *through* principle, to the Person of God Himself.

Too many people focus on God's *law*, and never see its extensions. They don't see what God's laws teach us about His character. The ultimate purpose of God in every precept is to bring us to the knowledge of Himself, because He desires a relationship with us. We can only know truth by knowing the God of truth.

You see, God's law is not an end in itself. Some of His commands were illustrative, others were practical, but all were—and are—an expression of His character. Note (in the spaces provided below) the qualities of God's commands, which King David extolled in *Psalm 19:7-9*:

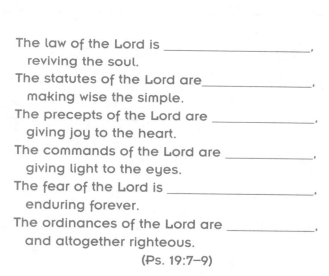

> The law of the Lord is _____,
>   reviving the soul.
> The statutes of the Lord are_____,
>   making wise the simple.
> The precepts of the Lord are _____,
>   giving joy to the heart.
> The commands of the Lord are _____,
>   giving light to the eyes.
> The fear of the Lord is _____,
>   enduring forever.
> The ordinances of the Lord are _____,
>   and altogether righteous.
>   (Ps. 19:7–9)

Note carefully the words David used to describe God's law: perfect, sure, right, radiant, pure, and righteous. Why do you think the law possesses those qualities? Because they are qualities that belong to the Lawgiver— God Himself. You see, the truth resides in the commands of God because they were given by the God of truth. The truth would not cease being true if the law were to disappear from the face of the earth, nor would it cease to be true if there were no humans to discern the principle—because the truth resides in the person of God Himself, who is eternal.

We can more effectively determine right from wrong when we look to God, His nature and character, as the measure of truth and morality. We can more consistently make right choices when we learn the process of truth—tracing the truth through the precept and principle to the person of God Himself.

The process of truth traces the truth through the precept and principle to the person of God.

Amanda's Second Chance

Do you think Amanda's conversation with her mother might have turned out differently if either Amanda or her mother had been able to see beyond the precept, through the principle behind the command and, ultimately, to the person of God Himself?

Write a new ending to that scene in the space allowed:

"What was so wrong? I went to a fun party and you had a relaxing evening at home, without worrying about your 'little lady.'"

"What was so wrong? We've taught you better than that. Lying is wrong, Amanda Lynn."

Now she was pulling the middle name stuff. Amanda hated her middle name; she thought it made her sound like a musical instrument, "a man-dolin."

"Why is it so wrong?" Amanda asked.

_____

_____

_____

_____

_____

_____

_____

_____

_____

Responding to the God of Truth

• How do you respond in your heart when you're confronted with the precepts of the Lord?

_____

_____

• How do you respond in your heart when you're confronted with the principles behind those precepts?

_____

_____

• How do you respond in your heart when you're confronted with the person of God Himself?

_____

_____

_____

_____

• Turn to *Exodus 33:13.* Do you understand any better today how learning "God's ways" can help you know Him and find favor with Him?

❏ Yes ❏ No

• Turn to *Psalm 19:7—9.* Use those verses as a guide for prayer; praise God for the qualities His law possesses (perfect, trustworthy, etc.), then pray through the verses again, praising Him because those are His attributes as well.

Truth and Consequences

Welcome to TV's most popular game show, in which contestants compete for fantastic awards and prizes!"

[Wild shouts and applause from the studio audience as cameras pan a brightly lit stage to the accompaniment of uptempo theme music.]

"And now, ladies and gentlemen, the host of Truth and Consequences, Tom Foolery!"

[More shouts and applause as handsome host jogs down the center aisle through the audience and leaps onto the stage, without mussing his hair.]

"Thank you, thank you, thank you."

[Foolery smiles broadly, revealing two perfect rows of white teeth, and speaks without moving his lips.]

"It's time for our first contestants. Let's give a Truth and Consequences welcome to Paul and Susan!"

[Two teenagers leap from their seats in the audience and jog down the aisle and up the steps to join Foolery on the stage. Foolery shoves a microphone under Susan's mouth.]

"Susan, tell us a little bit about yourself."

"Well, I'm a high school junior from Navajo, Idaho, and —"

"That's great, Susan!"

[Foolery glances at Paul's nametag and points the microphone his direction.]

"Where are you from, Paul?"

"Hi, Tom. I'm 15 years old, and I'm from Tuscaloosa, Alabama."

[Foolery smiles into the camera]

"Well, Paul, if my Tuscaloosa, I'd get it tightened."

[Riotous laughter wafts into the studio through loudspeakers. Foolery strides stage right, and motions for Susan and Paul to follow him.]

"Let's play Truth and Consequences. Our first game involves these two doors."

[He points to two large, brightly-colored doors on the stage. He pulls an index card from his pocket and begins to read.]

"You may choose the prize that's behind the red door or the prize behind the blue door. I'll even tell you what the prizes are."

[The sound of a drumroll enters the studio through the loudspeakers.]

"Behind the red door are two free tickets to next Saturday's Counting Cannibals concert. A group of your friends are already going, and you want to go, don't you?"

[Paul and Susan nod; the audience applauds.]

"But you don't have the money, do you?"

[Paul and Susan nod again; the audience applauds.]

"Behind the blue door is a night at home alone with your mom and dad watching a rerun of *Matlock*."

"I choose the red door!"

[The audience erupts in applause again as Paul and Susan simultaneously shout their response. Foolery flashes a toothy smile.]

"Not so fast. In order to open the red door, you must agree to 'borrow' $60 dollars from your mother's purse. . . after all, you didn't think we'd buy the tickets, did you? And, of course, you can always repay the money later."

[Laughter again wafts into the studio through the loudspeaker. Foolery continues speaking.]

"To open the blue door, simply don't 'borrow' the money. What'll it be, the concert of the year with all your friends. . . or *Matlock* with Mom and Dad?"

Red Door, Blue Door

What would you do? Which door would you choose?

    ❑ Red   ❑ Blue

Which would be the right choice, based on what you know now about the precepts, principles, and person of the God of truth?

    ❑ Red   ❑ Blue

Tom Foolery's little game illustrates the fact that, even when we measure right and wrong according to God's nature and character, it doesn't guarantee we will choose right. The battle isn't over when we discern what's right; we must still do what's right by committing to God's way.

That's not always easy, however. Many wrong choices offer immediate "gain," while right choices often seem to involve short-term "pain." Sin is often packaged very appealingly and carries a promise of instant gratification. Right choices, on the other hand, often require postponing immediate satisfaction for better long-term results.

> Right choices often require postponing immediate satisfaction for better long-term results.

Pain or Gain?

To be honest, if we make moral choices simply on the basis of what will bring immediate pain or gain, we will very often make the wrong choice.

We're not alone in that; it's been going on for centuries.

Unscramble the names of Bible characters below (if you have trouble, look up the Scripture passage for help). Then read the Scripture passages carefully and circle those who chose immediate gratification.

DAVE AND MAE _____ *(Gen. 3:1–7)*

OSMANS _____ *(Judg. 16:1)*

IDCUTJAR OASIS _____ (Matt. 26:14–16)

O J SHEP_____ (Gen. 39:1–10)

DAN VISE HAD BAD BATH _____ (2 Sam. 11:1–4)

INCAN BALADE _____ (Gen. 4:1–8)

CHANA _____ (Josh. 7:1)

VIDAD _____ (1 Sam. 26:1–11)

REFLECTION AND RESPONSE

• Which of the characters above do you identify with most?

_____

• Review the choices you have made today. Did you choose immediate gratification? Why or why not? _____

• List five or more situations this week in which you were faced with a moral choice, a choice to do right or to do wrong.

    I.

    2.

    3.

    4.

    5.

• In those situations, did you choose immediate gratification:

❑ all the time
❑ most of the time
❑ about half the time
❑ hardly ever
❑ never

• Since wrong choices so often seem to promise immediate "rewards," why would you ever make the right choice?

_____

_____

_____

_____

_____

_____

_____

_____

Why
Choose
Right?

• What can you say to God in response to what you're learning today?

_____

_____

_____

_____

_____

_____

_____

Why Choose Right?

d a y 5

"Time's up!"

[Truth and Consequences host Tom Foolery grins and raises his eyebrows. He addresses Paul and Susan.]

"What'll it be, kids? The red door. . ."

[He sweeps his hand toward the red door in a Vanna White gesture.]

"Or the blue door?"

[He waves at the blue door as if batting at a fly, and points the microphone at Susan.]

I'll take the red door."

[The audience applauds wildly; Foolery tips the microphone toward Paul.]

"Can I take the red door, too?"

"You sure can!"

[Foolery's grinning expression hasn't changed.]

"Well, then, I want the red door, too!"

[Audience claps and cheers, Foolery grins into camera, and theme music begins playing through the studio loudspeakers.]

"Congratulations, kids! You're going to the Counting Cannibals concert! And we're going to a commercial. We'll be back after these messages."

[Fade and out.]

Who Wouldn't Choose Red?

You might be saying, "Well, duh! Given a choice between a wrong choice that offers immediate rewards and a right choice that doesn't, why choose right?"

Fair question. In order to answer it, you have to realize that Tom Foolery didn't give Paul and Susan all the relevant information.

You see, a lot of people—Christians included—see God's commands as constricting. They think that biblical morality is confining. They don't see the benefits to a moral lifestyle. But God's commands, like those of a loving parent—"don't touch the stove," "look both ways before you cross the street," "eat your vegetables"—are not meant to spoil our fun and make us miserable.

God gave commands, such as "Flee sexual immorality," "Husbands, love your wives," "You shall not commit adultery," and all other commands because He wanted to protect us and provide for us. He didn't throw those precepts into the Bible just because He liked the way they sounded; He didn't concoct those rules to be a killjoy or to throw His weight around; He gave those commands because He knew some things we didn't. He knew, for example, that sexual immorality is a path, not to pleasure and fulfillment, but to emptiness and frustration.

Look at what Moses said about God's commands:

"And now, Israel, what does the Lord your God require from you, but to fear the Lord your God, to walk in all His ways and love Him, and to serve the Lord your God with all your heart and with all your soul, and to keep the Lord's commandments and His statutes <u>which I am commanding you today for your good</u>"? (Deut. 10:12–13, NASB).

According to that verse, why did God issue His commands? _____

_____

Looking down from an objective, universal, and eternal perspective, He could see things that we cannot, and He issued precepts to protect us and to provide for us.

Read *Jeremiah 29:11* and answer the following questions:

1. Who knows the plans God has for you?

_____

_____

2. What kind of plans are they?

_____

_____

3. Does this verse refer to God's protection and provision? How?

_____

_____

Next, turn another page or two in your Bible to *Jeremiah 32:39-41,* in which God talks about what He desires for those who follow Him.

1. Why does God want people to fear Him and obey Him?

_____

_____

"I know the plans I have for you," declares the Lord, "plans to prosper you and not to harm you, plans to give you hope and a future." Jeremiah 29:11

2. What does God rejoice in?

_____

_____

3. Do these verses make it sound like God wants to spoil your fun or prevent you from enjoying the best life has to offer?

❏ Yes   ❏ No

Now, all this doesn't mean that bad things won't happen to moral people, nor that immoral people are never happy. But God's commands mark the path to the greatest rewards.

For example, suppose Paul had chosen the blue door instead of imitating Susan's choice of the red door. She would have enjoyed the concert, and he would have endured a night of _Matlock_ with his parents. But though they may not have been so immediately gratifying, think about the benefits of his choice:

1. He would not have had to worry about his wrong choice being discovered.

2. He would not have had to wrestle with guilt.

3. He would have been able to face his mom without averting his eyes.

4. He would have bolstered his self-respect and self-esteem.

5. He would have contributed to a pattern of behavior that could earn him a reputation as a person of integrity.

6. And, who knows, his mom might have intended to use that $60 in her purse to buy him a new sports team jacket.

Long after the Counting Cannibals concert was over, Paul could have been enjoying the benefits of honesty—if he had made the right choice.

Choosing God's Protection and Provision

The research study that revealed the existence of "the club" clearly supports the notion that immoral behavior produces negative results. It indicates that moral behavior makes teens more likely to say they are satisfied with their lives, that they have high hopes, that they are respected by others. The study seems to show that right choices breed a healthy self-esteem, making kids more likely to think of themselves as "achievers."

Immoral behavior, on the other hand, fosters negative attitudes, making kids more likely to say they are "resentful," "lonely," "angry with life," "unmotivated," "disappointed," and "confused."

• Which long-term consequences would you prefer?

• List below the two rewards of right choices as revealed in this study:

God's _____

God's _____

• Have you enjoyed God's protection and provision as a result of choosing right? If so, describe it below:

_____

_____

_____

_____

_____

• Read *Jeremiah 29:11* again. Copy it below:

_____

_____

_____

_____

_____

_____

• Using *Jeremiah 29:11* as a guide, spend a few moments in prayer, thanking God for the plans He has for you.

week three week

week 3

week

Who's the Boss?

ho's the Boss? was the name of a popular American sitcom which ran for several years. The plot of the show involved a single-mother professional who hired a single father as a house-keeper and baby-sitter. The title apparently referred to the fact that employer and employee frequently became confused over their roles. The woman was in charge, but they often struggled to keep their nontraditional roles (and families) straight.

Something similar goes on between God and His creatures. . . well, okay, between Him and some of His creatures. It all started long before *Who's the Boss,* of course, long before TV. It began sometime before time.

The details are kind of sketchy, but a long time ago an archangel got a little confused about who was the boss. Okay, he got a lot confused.

He thought to himself, *"I will ascend to heaven; I will raise my throne above the stars of God; I will sit enthroned on the mount of assembly, on the utmost heights of the sacred mountain. I will ascend above the tops of the clouds; I will make myself like the Most High"* (Isa. 14:13-14). He thought things would be better if he were the one calling the shots. He figured he was as qualified as the next guy to be "Numero Uno." He wanted to be top dog.

Before he could implement his plan to promote himself to bosshood, however, the real Boss—God, the Most High—found out. . . and sent the archangel packing. Word has it that nowadays that archangel (who's been called Lucifer, Satan, and the devil, to name some of his nicer names) is trying to get men and women of all ages to imitate his disastrous mistake.

You'll learn more about that in this week's series of studies. . . and you'll also learn how to keep from making the fundamental mistake of for-getting (or denying) who's the Boss.

Adam's
Family

d a y 1

The snake snuck up behind the woman.

"Yo, Mama," he said (even though she wasn't a mother yet).

"How come you haven't tried that fruit tree at the center of the garden?"

"God said not to," she answered.

"He really said you couldn't eat from all these fruity trees?" He would have swept an arm around to indicate the many fruit trees that surrounded them, but serpents don't have arms.

"No," she answered. "He just said we couldn't eat from that tree—couldn't even touch it, I think He said, or we would die."

"Aw, you're kidding me! You won't die from touching that ol' tree. God just doesn't want you going near it because He knows if you eat that fruit you'll become like Him."

Eve looked puzzled.

"Hey, let me break it down for you, Mama, let me make it really simple. God is saying He's the only One who can define what is truly right and wrong. And, to make things worse, He's got the gall to try to impose it on you. That's not right, Mama. You have what it takes to determine for yourself what is good and evil. You don't have to accept His ideas. You can figure that out your own self. You can have it your way. You have the power to define truth within yourself—just like God does. Now doesn't that sound good?"

The serpent's spiel worked, of course, and Eve ate the fruit. But not only had the serpent convinced her that she was capable of judging good and evil, as we discussed above; he had also persuaded her to rebel against the Sovereign Lord, her Creator. He got her to willfully ignore God's precept ("You must not eat from the tree of the knowledge of good and evil"). Eve later induced her husband, Adam, to eat; got kicked out of the garden; and went on to raise Adam's family.

The Serpent's Technique

Read *Genesis 3:1-5,* and complete the following:

The serpent persuaded the woman to doubt God's precept. Write the verse below in which the tempter planted doubt in the woman's mind about the reasonableness of God's command:

_____

_____

_____

This Week's Verse—

Trust in the Lord
and do good;
dwell in the land and
enjoy safe pasture.
Delight yourself
in the Lord and
he will give you
the desires
of your heart.

Psalm 37:3-4

The serpent prompted the woman to doubt God's person. Write the serpent's words below that planted doubt in the woman's mind about God's truthfulness.

_____

_____

_____

_____

_____

The serpent induced the woman to doubt God's motivation. Write the serpent's words below that planted doubt in the woman's mind about God's motivation.

_____

_____

_____

_____

_____

Read *Genesis 3:6-10,23.* According to these verses, what were the first results of Adam and Eve's rebellion? (check all that apply)

- ❏ **they got food poisoning**
- ❏ **they experienced guilt and shame for the first time**
- ❏ **they invented applesauce**
- ❏ **they were kicked out of the garden**
- ❏ **they damaged their relationship with God**
- ❏ **they lost their purity, innocence, and happiness**
- ❏ **they decided never to trust a snake again**

Read *Genesis 3:11-13.* The man and the woman had similar reactions when God asked them what they had done. . . they tried to blame someone else.

Who did Adam try to blame?_____

Who did Eve try to blame?_____

God's Way or My Way?

Not much has changed since Adam and Eve. The devil still tries to get us to doubt God's precepts, and His person, and His motivation. We still suffer unhappy consequences from our wrong choices. And we try to excuse our wrong choices by:

- blaming someone else
- saying, "I didn't know it was wrong"
- claiming, "I had no choice"
- explaining that it really wasn't wrong in our case
- justifying our actions because they weren't as bad as what other people have done

But none of that really works. Because ultimately our struggles about right and wrong come down to a struggle between our way and God's way. The real issue usually isn't, "What's right and what's wrong?" but "Whose version of right and wrong will I accept—my own or God's?"

Satan, in the guise of a serpent, convinced Eve that it wouldn't be so bad to reject God's version of right and wrong in favor of her own customized version. But we know how well that turned out, don't we?

Decisions, Decisions

Are you willing to admit that God is the only Righteous Judge, and that He alone can decide right and wrong?

❏ Yes   ❏ No

Are you ready to submit to His version of right and wrong, and follow what He says is right?

❏ Yes   ❏ No

If your answer to both questions was "yes," you're ready to take the following steps of submission:

Admit that God is God.

1. Turn from your selfish ways (repent and confess your sin) and admit that God is God (*1 John 1:9*). Acknowledge that you have been living contrary to God's ways, that you have been trying to "do your own thing" and go your own way. Agree that your own way is wrong, and that God (and God alone) defines what is right and wrong.

Submit to God's way.

2. Submit to God as Savior and Lord and commit to His ways. If God can keep planets spinning in space, rivers running to the seas, and seasons coming and going, do you think He will mess up your life if you give Him control? Hand your life over to Him, and depend on Him for the power to make right choices. A simple, heartfelt prayer such as the following, can open your soul to the love and light of God:

Lord Jesus, I want to know You personally, the One who knows my future and has my best interest at heart. I realize that I am a sinner. Thank You for dying on the cross for my sins. I open the door of my life and trust You as my Savior and Lord. Thank You for forgiving my sins and giving me eternal life. Thank you for defeating death by coming out of the grave. Because You are the Living God take control of my life. By the power of your Holy Spirit, make me the kind of person You want me to be, and help me make the kind of choices You want me to make. Amen.

If you have already trusted Christ for salvation, but you've still been struggling (and often failing) to make right choices, the following prayer is suggested:

Father God, I need You. I acknowledge that I have been directing my life and that, as a result, I have sinned against You. I thank You that You have forgiven my sins through Christ's death on the cross for me. I now invite Christ to again take His place on the throne of my life. By the power of your Holy Spirit, enable me to commit to Your ways and make right choices in Jesus' name. Amen.

Trusting God to fill you with His Spirit doesn't mean that you will never again blow it through lack of faith or disobedience. But you can live more consistently day after day if you daily admit God's sovereignty, sincerely submit to His loving authority, and employ a simple process every time you face a choice. It's that process we will be discussing through the rest of this week.

Close today's study time in prayer, admitting God's sovereignty, submitting to His authority, and asking Him to guide you and speak to you the rest of this week through His Word.

Consider the Choice

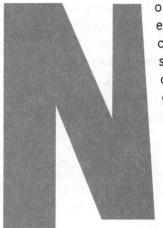

olo Buggins is only a half-millimeter tall. He never eats, and he never sleeps. He's a video-game character, like Sonic the hedgehog or M. Bison the street fighter. But Nolo's not happy in the world of computer-generated characters. He's tired of getting run over by Sonic and kicked and punched by Goro. He wants out.

Nolo can escape by navigating the video screen below, but it's a complicated maze filled with dangers and dead-ends. Give poor Nolo a hand; draw his escape route with a pencil or pen to help him escape from the violent, frenetic world of video games into a new, peaceful life as a church youth group leader.

day 2

FREEDOM!

2 TONS

OOPS!

THE PIT

NOLO'S PLACE

So how did it go? Did you succeed or fail in helping Nolo escape his video world?

Which of the following tactics did you use?

___ started at the end and worked my way to the beginning
___ paused to think ahead every time I was faced with a choice between two directions
___ hurried through without pausing or thinking
___ got my calculus teacher to do it for me

Consider the Choice

Nolo's little maze is like life in some ways. It's filled with decisions and dead ends. It's fraught with dangers. It can be frustrating, and it can be rewarding.

But most of us navigate Nolo's maze with more care and forethought than we give to the choices we face in life. Most of us complete a maze by pausing to think ahead every time we're faced with a choice between two directions. But we don't often do that in life.

An opportunity arises to copy Jennifer Tabuchi's algebra test answers, and we don't give it a thought. We just do it.

We have the chance to park in a dark place with our date, and we don't stop to think. We just do it.

We get invited to a party at the home of one of the most popular (and wildest) kids in school, and we don't hesitate. We just do it.

Every one of those "little" choices, however, like the frequent forks in Nolo's maze, represented a choice between the right path and the wrong path. Every decision represented an opportunity to select God's way or our own way. That's why the first step in submitting to God is to consider the choice.

Step 1:

Consider
the
Choice.

Joseph's Choice

Read *Genesis 39:1-10.* Then change the following statements to make them correct.

1. God blessed Andujar's household because of Joseph *(v. 5).*

2. Potiphar's wife noticed Joseph because he took steroids *(vv. 6-7).*

3. Joseph responded to his master's wife without thinking *(vv. 7-9).*

4. Joseph accepted the advances of Potiphar's wife because, he said, "No one is greater in this house than I am" *(vv. 8-9).*

5. Joseph had trouble seeing which choice would be right and which would be wrong *(vv. 8-9).*

6. Joseph had to face this temptation and make this choice once *(v. 10).*

Do you think Joseph considered the choice carefully? Or did he just make a decision suddenly, without any deliberation? _____

_____

What part of the passage *(Gen. 39:1-10)* supports your answer? _____

_____

What About You?

When you are faced with a moral choice, do you see it as a choice between going your way or God's way?

❏ Yes　❏ No　❏ Sometimes

Do you tend to consider the choice carefully or do you make a decision suddenly, without thinking? _____

_____

_____

_____

_____

What can you do in the future to consider the choice between your way and God's way? _____

_____

_____

_____

_____

_____

Turn to *Psalm 25:4-5.* Pray those words to God (several times if necessary), making them truly the prayer of your heart.

Compare It to God

So you submitted to God last week in youth group, and you've even begun to consider your choices a lot more than ever before. In the moment of decision you're learning to see simple everyday choices as opportunities to choose right or wrong.

You've made the first step in daily submitting your will to God and following His ways. The next step, after considering the choice—is to compare it to God.

In other words, after you weigh the choice you're facing in any situation, and acknowledge that it presents the opportunity to choose rightly or wrongly, you can proceed to compare your choice of action to the Person of God.

For example, when your brother begs you to cover for him by telling your parents he was with you last Friday night, you **(1) consider the choice,** recognizing it as an opportunity for a right or wrong decision, and **(2) compare it to God.**

When your dream date begins to grope, you **(1) consider the choice,** recognizing it as an opportunity for a right or wrong decision, and **(2) compare it to God.**

When the cafeteria lady at school undercharges you for lunch, leaving you enough to buy a can of soda, you **(1) consider the choice,** recognizing it as an opportunity for a right or wrong decision, and **(2) compare it to God.**

How do you compare it to God? By using the truth process you learned last week. Can you remember the three key words that express that process? Write them below:

P_____

P_____

P_____

Joseph's Standard

Turn again to *Genesis 39:1-10.* Read those verses again.

Although Joseph lived centuries before the Ten Commandments were given to the nation of Israel, his attitudes and actions reveal a strong knowledge of the precepts, principles, and Person of God.

Compare Joseph's situation with the Ten Commandments *(Ex. 20:1-17).* Which **precepts** would have applied to Joseph's situation? _____

_____

_____

Step 2:

Compare it to God.

_____

_____

_____

What godly **principles** would Joseph have violated if he had given in to Potiphar's wife?

_____

_____

_____

_____

In what ways was Joseph's behavior (toward Potiphar, toward Potiphar's wife, toward God Himself) like the **person of God?**

_____

_____

_____

What part of the scriptural account indicates that Joseph did, in fact, compare his action to the person of God?

_____

_____

_____

A View of You

The first two steps of submission to God, then, are:

C_____

C_____

Seems pretty simple, doesn't it? It's not that hard to remember. Of course, doing it is another matter.

Are you facing any choices right now to which you can apply these first two steps?

❏ Yes   ❏ No

If you answered "yes," complete the following statements:

If I look at this particular situation as an opportunity for doing right or doing wrong, I would _____

_____

_____

If I compare this particular action to the person of God, I would

_____

_____

Complete at least one of the following statements:

Here's what I'm thinking: _____

Here's what I'm feeling: _____

Here's what's bothering me: _____

Here's what I'm excited about: _____

Here's what I want to pray about: _____

Spend a few moments in prayer, using the following as a guideline:

- Talk to God honestly about the statements you've made above.
- Ask Him to give you patience and perseverance as you continue in this study.
- Pray for the needs and concerns of one other person in your youth group.

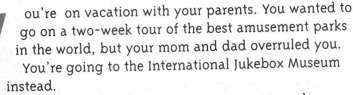

Commit to God's Way

You're on vacation with your parents. You wanted to go on a two-week tour of the best amusement parks in the world, but your mom and dad overruled you. You're going to the International Jukebox Museum instead.

You've been in the car with your parents and your little sister for four days, and if she sings the "Zoobilee Zoo" theme song one more time, you'll absolutely have to knock yourself unconscious against the window.

Your dad has stopped the car only once in those four days, announcing as you poured yourself out of the car, "We leave in exactly three minutes."

Lately, however, you've noticed that the scenery seems to be repeating itself. That restaurant sign advertising "blubbery pancakes" has gone by your window three times now, and your dad has folded and unfolded the map several times in the last few minutes, as if expecting something new to appear from its folds.

"Are we lost?" you ask.

"No," Dad says in a voice of exasperation. "We're almost there."

"Daddy, I have to go to the bathroom," your little sister says.

"It won't be long now, Sweetcakes," he says.

"Why don't you just ask directions?" your mom suggests.

"I don't need directions. I know where I'm going."

"That must explain," your mom says, pointing out the window, "why we've passed that little park four times now."

"All right, all right," your dad finally says. He jerks the car into a gas station, rolls his window down, and asks the man washing the windows for directions to the International Jukebox Museum.

"Right at the light," the man answers, popping his chewing gum in his cheek. "Two miles, hang a left at the bottling company. The next left is Jukebox Drive."

Your dad thanks the man, pulls out of the service station, and turns left at the next light.

"Dear," your mom says, "the man said to turn right at the light."

"I know."

"But you turned left back there," you say.

"I know."

"You're going the wrong way," Mom says.

"No," your dad answers. "I'll still get there. I'll just go my own way."

You slump back in your seat. Your sister starts singing "Zoobilee Zoo." You eye the window, wondering how hard you'd have to hit your head to knock yourself unconscious.

That's pretty unrealistic, isn't it? No one would get directions from someone who knows the way and then choose to ignore them. But we do

Step 3:

Commit to God's Way.

that all the time. God has given us directions in the form of precepts that point to principles that spring from His person. Yet we often choose to go our own way rather than follow directions from someone who knows the way. For that reason, even when we consider the choice and compare it to God, we still must commit to His way or we will go the wrong direction.

Joseph's Determination

Read *Genesis 39:1-12,* and afterward answer the following questions by circling T (true) or F (false).

T   F   Joseph had to face the temptation posed by Potiphar's wife many times.

T   F   Joseph didn't think what she had in mind was wrong; he just didn't find her attractive.

T   F   Joseph refused to go to bed with Potiphar's wife, but he still hung around with her.

T   F   Joseph's behavior shows that he was committed to obeying God.

T   F   Joseph committed to God's way because it was convenient.

T   F   Committing to God's way apparently meant to Joseph that he would try to do the right thing.

Joseph did the right thing in the face of unremitting temptation because he **considered the choice** as an opportunity to do right or wrong, **compared it to God** (recognizing that such behavior contradicted the nature and character of a God who is pure, faithful, and trustworthy), and **committed to God's way,** deciding that he would accept God's "directions" and adjust his behavior accordingly. Not only that, but *verse 10* makes it clear that he *planned* his behavior to help him commit daily to God's way.

Your Way, God's Way

Are you ready to commit to God's way? It's the kind of commitment you make once, and then make again every time you're faced with a moral choice. It means turning from your selfish ways and saying, "God, I see that Your way is right, and I commit to following You, with Your help, in the power of Your Holy Spirit."

If you are ready, why not put your commitment in writing, a kind of "manifesto," to guide you in your future decision-making. For example, if Joseph's commitment had been recorded, it might have looked like this:

"I commit to following God's way.
I will compare my choices with what I know of God's
nature and character;
I will avoid situations in which I know I could be tempted,
I will trust God to deliver me from temptation, and
I will run from evil when it appears, leaving even my
cloak behind if I must."

Get the idea? Use the lines below to record your own "manifesto," your own determination to commit to God's way.

_____

_____

_____

_____

_____

_____

_____

_____

_____

_____

_____

Now seal your commitment with a prayer to God, telling Him your determination, when faced with a moral choice, to:

Consider the choice
Compare it to God
Commit to God's way.

Count On It

Once you you have considered the choice, compared it to God, and then committed to God's way, there is one final step in the process of submitting to the Sovereign Lord, and that is to count on God's protection and provision.

When we humbly **admit** God's sovereignty and sincerely **submit** to His loving authority, we can not only begin to see clearly the distinctions between right and wrong, but we can also begin to count on God's protection and provision.

This doesn't mean that everything will be rosy; in fact, God says pretty bluntly that you may sometimes suffer for righteousness' sake. But even such suffering has rewards. Living according to God's way and allowing the Holy Spirit to live through you brings many spiritual blessings, like freedom from guilt, a clear conscience, the joy of sharing Christ, and (most importantly) the blessing of God upon your life.

You can also enjoy many physical, emotional, psychological, and relational benefits when you commit to God's ways. While God's protection and provision should not be the primary motivation for obeying God, it certainly provides a powerful encouragement for choosing right and rejecting wrong!

A Bum Rap

Ancient newspaper accounts (discovered by archaeologists from Central Bogus University) will help reveal the experience of one person who considered the choice, compared it to God, committed to God's ways, and counted on God's protection and provision.

HIGH OFFICIAL DISGRACED

MEMPHIS, EGYPT — Joseph ben Jacob, a civil servant in the Hyksos administration, was arrested this morning on charges that he assaulted the wife of an unnamed superior. Potiphar, the captain of the guard and investigating officer in the case, confirmed the report.

The wife, despite the trauma caused by her experience, initially reported the incident to her household servants. When her husband arrived home, she told him and presented evidence of the assault, a cloak her attacker left behind as he fled.

Joseph is being held without bail in the king's prison in Memphis. No trial date has been set.

Step 4:

Count on God's Protection and Provision.

AUTHORITIES WON'T REVEAL VICTIM'S IDENTITY

MEMPHIS, EGYPT — Government officials refused to release the name of the woman who accused Joseph ben Jacob of assault Tuesday, saying only that she is the trusted wife of an influential official.

Some highly placed sources report that the Queen and her entourage were away from the capital on a pleasure cruise down the Nile at the reported time of the incident, so the Queen is certainly not the victim.

Rumors in the halls of government place the wife of Potiphar, the captain of the guard, at the center of the story. She has so far refused to return calls.

ACCUSED HAS CHECKERED PAST

MEMPHIS, EGYPT — The non-Egyptian who yesterday was accused of assaulting a government official's wife allegedly has a record of violent encounters in the past.

Unnamed sources are quoted as saying that Joseph ben Jacob arrived in Egypt some years ago after narrowly escaping death in a family quarrel. After his own brothers imprisoned him (an act of mercy to avert execution for previous crimes), he was delivered from captivity by Potiphar, the arresting officer in this sordid case.

Joseph's own father is an acknowledged perjurer and extortionist, known to have built his ranching empire by stealing from his brother and father-in-law.

The family of the accused was last known to be living in tents and roaming the land of Canaan with their flocks of sheep.

Accused Maintains Innocence

MEMPHIS, EGYPT — Joseph ben Jacob, who lost his position yesterday as a trusted civil servant due to charges of assault, has steadfastly maintained his innocence, saying, "How could I do such a wicked thing and sin against God?"

Potiphar, who has not appointed an attorney to defend the accused, responded to reports of Joseph's statement by saying, "It's the word of a Hebrew servant against that of a government official's wife. Who would you believe?"

Compare the above accounts to *Genesis 39:13-20*.

I. What were the immediate results of Joseph's choice? (check all that apply)

❏ He was disgraced and imprisoned.
❏ He earned a guest appearance on "Fresh Prince of Bel Air."
❏ He was falsely accused of wrongdoing.
❏ He lost the trust of his boss.
❏ He accepted a position with a powerful government lobbying firm.

2. Do these accounts make it sound like Joseph enjoyed rewards for choosing to do right?

❏ Yes   ❏ No

3. Do you think the consequences of his actions made him sorry he had committed to God's way?

❏ Yes   ❏ No

Why or why not?_____

_____

Joseph's Reward

"Oh great," you may say. "What an endorsement for submitting all my decisions to God! 'Commit to God's way, get falsely accused of a terrible crime, go to prison'—where do I sign up?"

Well, now, hold on just a minute. That's not the end of the story. Remember, doing the right thing may not bring immediate rewards. But did Joseph suffer in the long run for committing to God's ways and following His directions? Let's see.

Read *Genesis 39:21-23.* What was Joseph's experience in prison? _____

_____

_____

Do you think the integrity he displayed in his former position helped him earn the prison warden's confidence?

❏ Yes   ❏ No

Why or why not? _____

Read *Genesis 41:38-52.* What benefits did Joseph eventually enjoy as a result of God's protection and provision? (check all that apply)

❏ wisdom   ❏ Sega video game
❏ integrity   ❏ paid holidays
❏ power   ❏ authority
❏ a new car   ❏ a clear conscience
❏ wealth   ❏ the favor of God
❏ a good reputation
❏ a wife and children

Responding to the Four Cs

There you have it. . . the four Cs for submitting every decision—not just daily, but hourly decisions—to the Sovereign Lord who knows you, who knows the future, and who knows what's best.

Write the four steps for making right choices from memory below:

4Cs

C_____

C_____

C_____

C_____

As you continue in this study, you're going to use the "4C" process over and over again. Right now, however, give some thought to what you've learned this week.

1. Do you have trouble with any of the 4Cs?

❏ Yes   ❏ No

If yes, which one? _____

2. Read *Psalm 37:3-6. Verses 3,4,* and *5* begin with similar phrases. Copy them below:

_____ in the Lord. . .

_____ in the Lord. . .

_____ to the Lord. . .

3. What kind of protection and provision will follow that kind of commitment?

He will _____ *(v. 4)*

He will _____

_____*(v. 6)*

4. Read those verses again, changing the words to reflect your commitment and trust (for example, you might pray, "I trust in You, Lord. I want to do good . . . and I trust You to make my righteousness shine like the dawn. . .").

week

week

week 4

week

Air Jordan

never would have believed it if I hadn't seen it!"

Two doctors stood in the hospital hallway. One just emerged from the delivery room; he removed a green mask from his face. The other stopped to listen to his friend's story.

"What wouldn't you believe?" the second doctor asked.

"The baby I just delivered. I've never seen anything like it!"

"Like what?"

"Well," the first doctor said, "I pulled the little guy out, you know, no problem. . ."

"Yeah?"

"Cut the umbilical cord. . ."

"Yeah," the other said, impatience creeping into his voice.

"And then I handed the kid to his father, who set the little tyke down on the floor."

"He laid a newborn baby on the floor?"

"I didn't say he laid him down. He just set him down. . . on his feet. And the kid stood there for a few seconds."

"A newborn baby stood up by himself?" The second doctor shook his head and then looked suspiciously at his friend. "You're pulling my leg."

"No, I'm serious! He stood right there on that delivery room floor, just like he'd been doing it all his life."

"Then what happened?"

"You won't believe it. He picked a cotton ball off the floor, tossed it in the air and caught it a couple times, and then made a mad dash for the trash can."

"He ran? You must think I'm some kind of fool."

"No, no, it's true. And when he got to the trash can—which was about four times his height—he leaped, twisted his body in the air, extended his arms, and dunked that little piece of cotton like it was a basketball!"

"Yeah, yeah. Real funny." The second doctor started to walk away.

"I'm not playing around!" the first doctor shouted after his departing friend. "I saw it with my own two eyes. This Michael Jordan kid is incredible!"

That story is ridiculous, of course. Michael Jordan may be among the greatest athletes of all time, but he still had to learn to stand, and walk, and run as a child. He even had to learn how to play basketball, just like everyone else. By the time he retired from basketball to pursue a baseball career, Jordan had set all kinds of records and helped his team win three straight championships.

It's amazing what practice can do. It can make a difficult game look easy. It can make a complex skill seem effortless. It can make a process of several steps feel natural.

That's what this week's studies are all about. You'll practice applying the **4Cs** to a real-life situation in which you must decide which action would be right and which would be wrong. . . and which you would choose. That can be even harder than sinking a half-court shot with one second left in the game.

Final Conflict

Dan barely made it to his chemistry exam. His mom had been in the hospital for four days now, and he'd been spending every waking moment at her bedside. He hadn't even heard the alarm go off this morning; by the time he awoke, it was 7:23 a.m. His chemistry final started at 8:05.

He slipped into his seat just as the tardy bell rang and breathed a weary sigh.

Ever since Mom's been sick, he thought, *I haven't been able to study like I should.*

He'd carried all *As* and *Bs* until the most recent grading period, but his grades had deteriorated since his mother had been hospitalized with cancer. He just didn't have the energy, it seemed, to study *and* take care of his mom.

So far he'd passed all his classes at least. But Mr. Henderson, his chemistry teacher, had this rule. You could get straight *As* all year, but if you flunked the last semester, you flunked the course. Dan had gotten *Bs* from Mr. Henderson so far, but he knew he wasn't ready for this final.

As he started the four-page final, Dan repeatedly shook his head, trying to clear the cobwebs that seemed to hide the answers.

I know this stuff, he told himself. *I know I do. I just can't think straight these days.*

He trudged through page after page, alternately hopeful and despairing of his chances at passing the test and the course.

He was beginning page three when Stephanie Andrews dropped a page from her test. It floated into the aisle and landed on the floor beside his chair. He glanced at Stephanie; she seemed not to notice, but something in the movement of her head suggested that the dropped page had not been an accident.

Stephanie had been a good friend to Dan. She had even visited his mom in the hospital. He looked from Stephanie to the others in the room. No one seemed to be paying any attention. Mr. Henderson sat at his desk in the corner of the room, only occasionally looking up from the papers he was grading.

Dan's eyes settled on Stephanie's neat handwriting. He could read the answers without difficulty. Dan's gaze returned to his own desk. He stared at the blank spaces on his test paper.

He began jotting the answers rapidly onto his own test. It was his only chance at passing the test—and the course, he figured. And it was only one page.

I knew those answers anyway, he told himself as he picked the page off the floor and handed it back to a sweetly smiling Stephanie. *I was just having trouble remembering them because of all that stuff with Mom. It's not like I'm cheating or anything. Not with everything I've had to worry about this month.*

This Week's Verse—

Daniel resolved not to defile himself with the royal food and wine, and he asked the chief official for permission not to defile himself this way.
Daniel 1:8

You Make the Call

What would you do—realistically—in that situation?

Do there seem to be compelling reasons—good reasons—for making one choice or the other? List those reasons below:

Reasons to use the answers he read on Stephanie's paper:

_____

_____

_____

_____

_____

_____

Reasons not to use the answers he read on Stephanie's paper:

_____

_____

_____

_____

_____

_____

What do you think is motivating Dan in the situation above? (check any that apply)

❏ A concern for his grades
❏ Convenience
❏ His own selfish interests
❏ Worry for his mother

- ❑ A desire to do the right thing
- ❑ Thought for his college plans
- ❑ Consideration for Stephanie's feelings
- ❑ A desire to make his mom proud of him
- ❑ An unwillingness to hurt Stephanie's feelings

If you were in Dan's situation, what would you do?

_____

_____

_____

Why would you do that?

_____

_____

_____

A Look at the Book

There's no Bible verse that says, "Dan shalt not copy from Stephanie's paper." There's no verse that says, "Dan shall copy from Stephanie's paper," either.

How would you decide, then, which choice was right in the above situation? After all, it can't be wrong to spend time visiting with a sick mother in the hospital, can it? It can't be wrong to accept help from a friend, can it?

Can you think of any Bible verses or passages that might apply to Dan's situation? List the verses or situations that you can think of.

_____

_____

_____

Even if you can't think of any verses, can you think of any biblical concepts or principles that might apply? If so, what are they?

_____

_____

_____

_____

If you have a study Bible or a Bible with a concordance, try using the concordance or topical index to help you answer the above questions.

As you prepare for this week's study, it is crucial that you be honest and realistic about what choices you would make—and why. To help you do that, check off any statements below that are true of you.

❏ I admit that I would probably behave like Dan in a similar situation.
❏ I honestly don't think I would copy Stephanie's answers.
❏ I would do whatever was easiest.
❏ I would feel bad about my choice.
❏ I probably wouldn't feel bad about my choice.
❏ I would ask God to forgive me if I was doing wrong.
❏ I would ask God to help keep me from doing wrong.

Now, in the space below, compose a prayer to God below based on the things you've said above, being careful to be honest with Him about your feelings and your actions.

Dan's Head

Dan, of course, is making a decision in a split second. He doesn't have time to check a Bible concordance and read through a workbook on right choices. That's usually the way things are. Decisions about right or wrong are most often the result of a moment's thought or a split—second impulse.

Still, an amazing number of thoughts and impulses take place in that short amount of time. Through the miracle of modern science, we can take a peek into Dan's head and see the high-speed processes that took place just before his decision to copy the answers from Stephanie's paper:

day 2

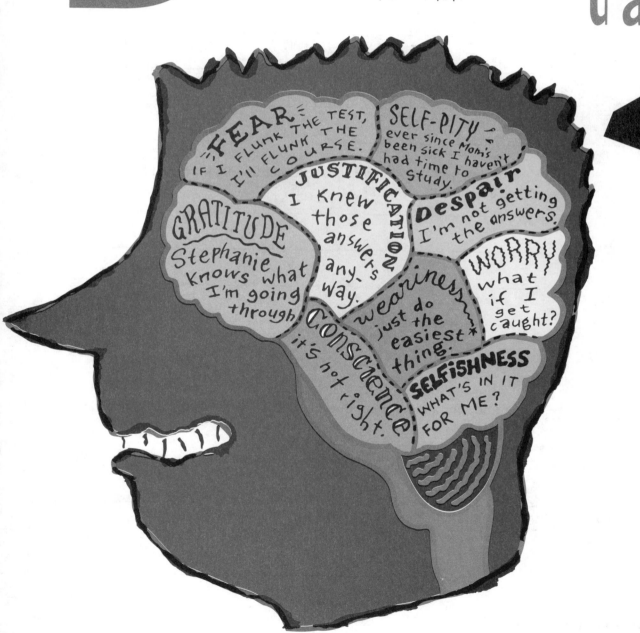

FEAR = IF I FLUNK THE TEST, I'll FLUNK THE COURSE.

SELF-PITY = ever since Mom's been sick I haven't had time to study.

JUSTIFICATION I knew those answers any- way.

DESPAIR I'm not getting the answers.

GRATITUDE Stephanie knows what I'm going through.

WORRY what if I get caught?

weariness just do the easiest thing.

CONSCIENCE it's not right.

SELFISHNESS WHAT'S IN IT FOR ME?

The 4Cs apply to
every area of
decision making.

If the human mind can process all that information in seconds, it can certainly handle the 4C process. In fact, the 4C process can actually streamline your decision-making, because it sorts all the various impulses and thoughts that assail your mind in a moment of decision.

So let's apply the 4C process to Dan's decision.

Consider the Choice

What Dan was doing in that chemistry final was evaluating the rightness or wrongness of his action based on the immediate benefits each action offered. That's only natural, of course.

What are some of the short-term benefits Dan might enjoy as a result of copying Stephanie's answers?

_____

_____

_____

_____

_____

What are some short-term consequences Dan might face if he had not copied Stephanie's answers?

_____

_____

_____

_____

_____

But now for an important question: do those considerations make Dan's decision right?

❏ Yes, because _____

_____

❏ No, because _____

_____

You see, Dan made a fundamental mistake. He tried to judge right and wrong (which is objective) by his experience (which was subjective). He let his situation cloud his judgment of right and wrong.

Turn to the drawing of Dan's head on page 71. Use a pencil to shade in any sections that reveal a reliance on an objective, universal, and constant standard of truth.

That's why the first step in making right choices—consider the choice—is so important, because it can immediately clear a mind clouded by a confusing and unpleasant situation. It can remind you that your choice is not between what you think is right and what you think is wrong; it's between what is objectively right and what is objectively wrong, regardless of what you think.

Another Dan

The Bible contains the story of another Dan who faced a difficult decision in an awkward situation. He and his Jewish friends were expected to eat what everyone else in the Babylonian palace ate. . . but the palace cafeteria apparently served food that God had forbidden *(Dan. 1:8)*.

After reading *Daniel 1:1-20,* write the thoughts in the picture below that you think might have dominated Daniel's head as he decided what he and his friends should do.

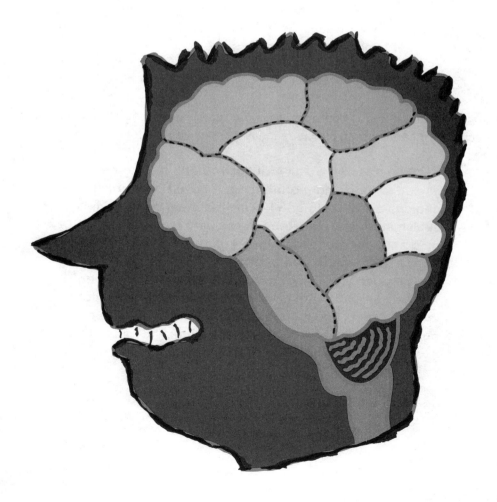

Did Daniel try to judge right and wrong (which is objective) by his experience (which was subjective)?

❏ Yes ❏ No

Do you think he considered the choice as a choice between what was objectively right and what was objectively wrong, regardless of what he thought or felt?

❏ Yes ❏ No

Consider Yourself

What about you? If you could buy a special mirror that allowed you to look into your own head, what would it reveal? Would it show:

❏ That you make decisions based on the immediate benefits?
❏ That you act according to what's in it for you?
❏ That you try to judge right and wrong by your experience, according to each situation?
❏ That you make choices based on an objective, universal, constant standard of right and wrong?

If you sincerely want to make right choices, choices that will please God and truly benefit you, how must you begin? By:

C_____ the C_____

If you are willing to continue in the process of submitting to God, who alone decides right and wrong, conclude today's study with the following prayer:

> Father God, I admit that I have been relying on myself to judge right and wrong. I have been making choices based only on what immediately benefits my selfish interests. I have been allowing my situation to guide my decisions, and then trying to call my choice "right." Help me to begin today to consider the choice, to view each moment of decision as a choice between what is right and what is wrong, independently of what I think or feel. I know I'll need Your Spirit's guiding presence to do that, so I again affirm my trust in You, in Jesus' name. Amen.

Reverse Action

**H**ave you ever watched a home movie or video run in reverse? It can be hilarious to watch people walking backwards, divers jumping magically out of a swimming pool and onto the diving board, and kids lighting the candles on a birthday cake by inhaling!

Wouldn't it be nice to do the same thing in real life? You could rewind the film of your life and take back that awful thing you said to Mrs. Huffenpuff. You could reverse your decision to eat cotton candy and a chili dog before riding the roller coaster. You could save yourself the embarrassment of that pathetic haircut you got at Dion's House of Hair.

Of course, real life doesn't have a rewind button. But Dan, the guy who copied Stephanie Andrews' test answer on the chemistry final, isn't real! So we can push rewind for him and examine what might have happened if he had submitted to God, using the 4Cs, instead of trying to make his own decision about right and wrong based solely on his situation.

If Dan had considered the choice, he could have recognized that his choice was not between what he thought was right or wrong, but between what *was* right or wrong, independently of his particular situation. He could then have proceeded to the next step in making right choices.

Compare It to God

What would have happened if Dan had compared his choice to the nature and character of God? What could he have learned by tracing his choice through precept and principle to the person of God?

Precept

Read *Leviticus 19:11.* How do those precepts apply to Dan's situation?

_____

_____

_____

Read Jesus' response to the Rich Young Ruler's question about eternal life in *Mark 10:19* and complete the phrase that applies to Dan's situation:

> "You know the commandments: 'Do not murder, do not commit adultery, do not steal, do not give false testimony, do not _____, honor your father and mother.'"

Read the following verses and then write the two-word phrase that appears in each verse:
1 Timothy 3:8; Titus 1:7; Titus 1:11

How do those verses apply to Dan's situation? _____

_____

_____

_____

Principle

What positive principle do you think lies behind each of those precepts? In other words, what attribute does God want us to possess that such behavior would contradict? (Hint: *Prov. 12:22* refers to this principle)

_____

_____

_____

Person

What is it, then, about God that the precepts and the principle point to? Is there something in God's nature and character that would make Dan's decision to copy Stephanie's answers wrong?

Read the following Bible verses and complete the statement that follows.

2 Samuel 7:28   God is _____

John 3:33   God is _____

Psalm 31:5   God is the God of _____

If Dan's head were filled with the 4Cs instead of the confusing and competing thoughts and feelings prompted by his situation, he would be able to see that to copy Stephanie's answers would be wrong, regardless of how tired he is, regardless of how life is treating him, regardless of Stephanie's willingness to help. His action would be wrong because, if you compare it to God, you will discover that:

- God's precepts forbid dishonest gain.

- God's precepts forbid dishonest gain because God values honesty and trustworthiness.

- God values honesty and trustworthiness because God is trustworthy and true.

The Pause Button

If you could rewind the tape of your life, would you reverse a recent decision you've made?

❑ Yes   ❑ No

How would you see things differently if you consider the choice in that situation and compare it to God?

_____

_____

_____

_____

Take a few moments to pray, committing that situation to God, asking Him for forgiveness (if necessary), and asking Him to guide you in future decisions through the 4Cs.

Dan Again

day 4

Dan dashed into his chemistry final and slid into his seat just as the tardy bell rang. He breathed a weary sigh.

Suddenly, a spooky feeling rushed over him, an overwhelming sense of *deja vu*. He felt as if someone had just punched some sort of cosmic rewind button. He felt as if he were reliving today's events.

The eerie feeling continued as Mr. Henderson distributed the four-page chemistry final with directions to keep the test face-down on the desk until he gave the signal to begin.

Dan found it difficult to concentrate on the test. *I know this stuff,* he told himself, but his sense that something weird was happening (along with fatigue from having spent so much time with his sick mother at the hospital) clouded his mind until he was convinced he would fail the exam.

He was beginning page three when Stephanie Andrews dropped a page from her test. It floated into the aisle and landed on the floor beside his chair. Now he knew something strange was going on; this had all happened to him before, he was sure of it.

He glanced at Stephanie; she seemed not to notice, but something in the movement of her head suggested that the dropped page had not been an accident. He was convinced that she intended for him to see her answers.

It would be so easy. His eyes settled on Stephanie's neat handwriting. He could read the answers without difficulty. His gaze returned to the blank spaces on his own test sheet.

Dan's sense of *deja vu* evaporated, however, when he closed his eyes to think. He considered what he was tempted to do, reminding himself that whatever he did, there was a right thing to do and a wrong thing to do, and that the decision was up to him.

In a moment, he remembered that God had forbidden lying and cheating; he couldn't recall any specific verse of Scripture, but he knew that God valued honesty and integrity—because God Himself was faithful and true.

Dan's mouth closed tightly as he realized beyond a shadow of a doubt that copying Stephanie's answers would be the wrong thing to do.

But, he told himself, *if I do the right thing, I could flunk the exam—and the course. And I sure don't want that to happen.*

Commit to God's Way

Unlike the rest of us, Dan has a second chance to make the right choice. But even though we've rewound the tape of his life, and even though he's **considered the choice** and **compared it to God,** he's not "home free". . . he still must **commit to God's way.**

What might committing to God's way involve for Dan in the above situation? (check all that you think apply)

❏ A quick prayer to God.
❏ A long prayer to God.
❏ Return the paper to Stephanie.
❏ Copy Stephanie's answers.
❏ Copy someone else's answers.
❏ Ask Mr. Henderson for hints.
❏ Ask God for hints.
❏ Try his hardest to pass the test on his own merits.
❏ Fake sickness.
❏ Fake death.
❏ Plan to take chemistry in summer school if necessary.
❏ Protest Mr. Henderson's stupid rule to the school board.
❏ Explain his mother's situation to Mr. Henderson and ask for a chance to retake the exam or complete extra work to improve his grade.
❏ Explain his mother's situation and offer to wash Mr. Henderson's car for the rest of his life.
❏ Resolve to do the right thing if it benefits him.
❏ Resolve to do the right thing regardless of the benefits or consequences.

We must admit that God is God and submit to Him.

If Dan is to make the right choice, he must admit that his choice is a choice between a real right and a real wrong, submit to God as the Authority who determines what is right or wrong, *and commit* to God's way by conforming to what God says is right, regardless of the benefits or consequences.

Another Daniel, Another Test

Reread *Daniel 1:1-20*. Do you see any similarities between Daniel's situation (in the Bible) and Dan's temptation (in this book)? If so, list the parallels below:

Dan   **Daniel**

How do you think Dan's situation would have ended if he had committed to God's way, like Daniel did? Try writing a new ending to Dan's story below.

_____

_____

_____

_____

_____

_____

_____

_____

_____

_____

_____

_____

_____

_____

_____

_____

_____

_____

Can you think of any situation in your life that would have ended differently if you had committed to God's way? If so, describe it here:

_____

_____

_____

_____

_____

_____

_____

_____

_____

Have you already committed to submitting to God, either in your youth group or during your daily sessions in this Workbook?

❏ Yes   ❏ No

If you have already made such a commitment, renew it now, perhaps repeating the "manifesto" you composed (p. 60) as a closing prayer to God.

If you have not made such a commitment, why not do so now? Admit God's sovereignty, and submit your will to Him, using the steps on pages 50-51.

Flunking and Passing

day 5

Dan sighed and leaned forward to pick Stephanie's test paper off the floor. He extended it toward her without looking at it.

Stephanie turned and met his gaze. She accepted the page without speaking.

Dan struggled through the exam, working hard to concentrate, skipping portions of the test that mystified him and concentrating his energies on areas in which he felt the most confident. He remained at his desk after most students—including Stephanie—had turned their tests in. He checked his work and attempted to complete the portions he'd skipped earlier.

He found out two days later: he had flunked the exam. He went to Mr. Henderson and begged him to waive his rule, or let him retake the exam; the teacher refused both requests.

Dan sat beside his mother's hospital bed, wondering if he should have just copied Stephanie's answers and saved himself all this trouble. He knew now that he would have passed the test with that little bit of help.

He looked at his mother's sleeping form, and shook his head. He had flunked one test, he realized, but he had passed another.

Counting On God's Protection and Provision

What were the immediate results of Dan's right choice? List them below:

_____

_____

_____

Do you think the results are immediately positive or negative? _____

The last of the 4Cs, you'll remember, is to **count on God's protection and provision.** What kinds of protection and provision could possibly result from Dan's choice above?

_____

_____

Dan may not instantly realize many of the benefits of making the right choice. But if Dan commits to God's way and then counts on God's loving protection and provision, even thanking God in faith before he sees any fruits of his obedience, he will pave the way for a much happier and healthier future.

Why? Because *God's standard of honesty provides a clear conscience, and an unbroken relationship with God.* If he had cheated on his chemistry final, Dan would have damaged his walk with God. With every right choice, Dan preserves and enriches his relationship with God.

God's standard of honesty protects from guilt. Guilt is among the most powerful of emotions, and it will cling to the dishonest heart like a python, choking the life out of its victim. The psalmist David realized the power of guilt, and expressed it in *Psalm 38:4;* read that verse and copy it below:

_____

_____

_____

Because Dan committed to God's way, he is protected from the burden of guilt.

God's standard of honesty provides a sense of accomplishment that the dishonest heart will never enjoy. It may take longer and involve sacrifice, but when Dan finally passes chemistry, it will be an accomplishment of which he can be proud, because it will belong only to him.

God's standard of honesty protects from shame. What would have happened if Dan had tried to copy Stephanie's answers and been caught? Even if he hadn't been caught, would Stephanie have respected him more or less for what he did? He'll never have to find out, because his choice protects him from shame.

God's standard of honesty provides a reputation for integrity. Dan may not realize it, but every time he makes a moral choice, he is building a reputation (either a good one or a bad one). Choosing God's way builds a reputation for integrity. Read *Proverbs 22:1* and copy its words below:

_____

_____

_____

When we **consider the choice, compare it to God,** and **commit to God's way,** we can **count on all the benefits of His protection and provision.**

Daniel's Band

Read *Daniel 1:1-13* in your Bible. Do you think Daniel was counting on God's provision and protection? If so, why?

_____

_____

Read *Daniel 1:14-16.* Did God's provision fulfill Daniel's expectations? If so, how?

_____

_____

Read *Daniel 1:17-20.* What long-term benefits did Daniel and his friends enjoy, in addition to passing their 10-day test?

_____

_____

_____

Beginning Now

Write the four steps for making right choices from memory below:

4Cs

C_____

C_____

C_____

C_____

What do you think would happen if you began now to choose God's way and count on His protection and provision? (check all that apply)

❏ He would disappoint me.
❏ He would make me miserable.
❏ He would protect me.
❏ He would embarrass me in front of my friends.
❏ He would provide for me.
❏ He would make me sorry I trusted Him.

Use the following (based on *Ps. 26:2-3*) as a model (changing it to express your own thoughts and feelings) to guide you in prayer to God:

> Test me, O Lord, and try me today. Examine my heart and my mind, and help me to be honest with You and with myself today. Your love is ever before me, and I thank You because Your motivation is always to protect me and provide for me. I want to walk continually in Your truth. Overcome all the obstacles in my heart and mind and let me submit to You completely, and commit to Your way, not my own, in Jesus' name. Amen.

week 5

Hot Topics

n the fifties, the shocking moves and music of a singer named Elvis Presley became a hot topic among preachers.

In the sixties, preachers were often asked what they thought about the "Jesus movement," in which large numbers of "hippies" and (believe it or not) "yippies" began professing faith in Christ.

In the seventies and eighties, many preachers were asked for their reactions to the fortunes and failures of television evangelists.

In Jesus' day, the hot topic of the day was none of the above. They didn't know who Elvis Presley was. They'd never heard of hippies. Television hadn't yet been invented. The question that made the rounds of teachers and preachers of Jesus' time was: "Which is the greatest commandment?"

An expert in the Law once came to Jesus with that question. He was a Pharisee, a group of people who knew the commandments inside and out; they believed that there was a commandment to cover every detail of life.

"Teacher," the man said, "which is the greatest commandment in the Law?"

Jesus answered, *"'Love the Lord your God with all your heart and with all your soul and with all your mind.' This is the first and greatest commandment. And the second is like it: 'Love your neighbor as yourself.' All the Law and the Prophets hang on these two commandments"* (Matt. 22:37-40).

In other words, Jesus was saying that everything God has revealed to us about right and wrong, all the dos and don'ts of His commandments and all the shalts and shalt-nots, are simply explanation and amplification of His command to love.

That question—and Jesus' answer—will be crucial to your discoveries and decisions this week as you continue applying the 4C process to the kinds of choices you must face every day.

Opportunity Knocks

onica turned to her mother and screamed. "Stop the car!"

Mrs. Jackson slammed her foot on the brakes, watching in the rear-view mirror as a rusty brown pickup truck stopped just in time to avoid a collision. She turned to her daughter, who sat beside her in the front seat.

"What's wrong?" Mrs. Jackson expected Monica to say they had almost run over an animal, but Monica pressed her face against the window and pointed at the line outside the movie theater.

"That's Jimmy," she whispered, "in line with Susan Brock."

Mrs. Jackson's eyes widened. "You mean I almost had an accident because you saw some old boyfriend going to the movies with someone else?"

Monica rolled her eyes without turning to face her mother. She just didn't understand. Jimmy wasn't just "some old boyfriend." It had been months now since her former friend, Gina Price, had broken them up and stolen Jimmy away. Jimmy and Gina had been going together ever since. And now he was in line at the movies with pretty Susan Brock.

"Monica Jackson!" Her mother was still stewing over her near-accident. "Don't ever do that to me again. Do you hear me?"

"Yeah, Mom," Monica muttered, still watching Jimmy and Susan. "I'm sorry."

Jimmy, who was ahead of Susan in line, had turned away from her and was now talking with Nate and Alex, two of his closest buddies. As her mom began to pull the car back into traffic, Monica saw that Jimmy was there with his friends, and Susan was accompanied by her parents. They weren't there together at all.

Too bad, she thought as she turned around and settled back into the seat. *Then Gina would know how it feels to have someone steal your boyfriend.*

An idea began to form in her head. *After all, she did see Jimmy at the movies with Susan. It wouldn't be lying to tell her former friend what she saw. And if she assumed that Jimmy was going out on her. . .* She smiled. *It was a golden opportunity. Besides, she needs to know how bad she hurt me. Then maybe she'd think twice before doing it again.*

Monica's Choice

Monica is not planning to lie to her "former friend." She's simply planning to tell Gina what she saw—that Jimmy and Susan were standing in line together at the movies.

day 1

This Week's Verse—

Eagerly desire the greater gifts. And now I will show you the most excellent way.
1 Corinthians 12:31

Have you ever been in a situation like Monica's, in which a friend hurt you or did something unkind to you? If you have, describe it in a few words below:

_____

_____

_____

_____

_____

Based on your experience, do you think Monica's reaction is natural?

❏ Yes   ❏ No

If you were in a similar situation, what do you think you would do?

_____

_____

_____

_____

Why would you do that? _____

_____

_____

Word to the Wise

Of course, there's no Bible verse that says, "Thou shalt not tell thy friend that thou sawest the boyfriend thy friend stole from thee standing in line at the movie theater with another girl."

How would you decide, then, which choice was right in a situation like Monica's? After all, it can't be wrong to tell a "former friend" the plain truth, can it? Besides, Monica's plan could teach Gina a valuable lesson.

Can you think of any Bible verses or passages that might apply to Monica's situation? If so, what are they?

_____

_____

_____

_____

Can you think of any biblical concepts or principles that might apply? If so, what are they?

_____

_____

_____

_____

If you have a study Bible or a Bible with a concordance, use the concordance or topical index to help you answer the above questions.

As you prepare for this week's study, it is crucial that you be honest and realistic about what choices you would make—and why. To help you do that, check off any statements below that are true of you.

- ❏ I have done something similar, like when I _____.
- ❏ I would never do something like what Monica is planning.
- ❏ I would probably feel like doing it, but I wouldn't go ahead with it.
- ❏ I would do whatever was easiest.
- ❏ I would do it, but I would feel bad about my choice.
- ❏ I would do it, and I probably wouldn't feel bad about my choice.
- ❏ I would do it and be proud of it.
- ❏ I would ask God to forgive me if I was doing wrong.
- ❏ I would ask God to help keep me from doing wrong.

What do you think God thinks about your answers above? Is He pleased with your honesty? Do you think He wishes any of your answers were different? Is His Spirit prodding your heart and your conscience about any of your answers?

Pray the words of _Psalm 139:23-24_ as you prepare your heart and mind for the coming week's studies and discoveries.

Monica's Move

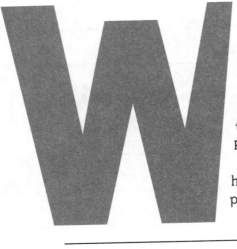

day 2

Who can blame Monica for what she's planning? It would be different, of course, if Gina had never done anything to her, right? It's like a game of chess, and Monica figures it's just her turn.

Put yourself in Monica's shoes. It would be awfully hard to say that giving Gina a taste of her own medicine was wrong. Right?

After all, she has some justification for her plan. List the things below that make her plan seem right:

_____

_____

_____

_____

Not only that, but anyone can see that she would enjoy some immediate benefits as a result of her plan. What would such benefits be?

_____

_____

_____

But now for that important question: do those things make Monica's plan right?

❑ Yes, because _____

❑ No, because _____

You see, Monica is trying to judge right and wrong (which is objective) by her emotions (which are subjective). She is letting her feelings cloud her judgment of right and wrong.

Consider the choice.

Rather than justifying her actions and proclaiming them "right" because of what Gina has done to her, Monica would be much better off to **consider the choice.** Monica should remember that her choice is not between what she thinks is right or what she thinks is wrong, but between what is right or wrong, regardless of what she thinks.

David's Move

Monica is not the first to face such a tempting opportunity. The Bible tells the story of David, who had been wronged by a former friend named Saul. In fact, Saul had actually tried to kill David (*1 Sam. 18:10-11; 19:1*).

Read *1 Samuel 26:1-25* and answer the following questions.

Do you think David's experience was similar in any way(s) to Monica's? If so, in what ways?

_____

_____

Do you think David tried to judge right and wrong (which is objective) by his emotions (which were subjective)?

❑ Yes   ❑ No

Can you cite any specific portions of the scriptural account to support your conclusion? If so, what are they?

_____

_____

Consider Yourself

What about you?

- Are you still making choices based on the immediate benefits?
- Are you justifying decisions about what's right or wrong according to what's in it for you?
- Are you trying to judge right and wrong by your emotions?
- Or are you beginning to consider the choice, making choices based on a belief in an objective, universal, constant standard of right and wrong?

If you sincerely want to make right choices, choices that will please God and truly benefit you, how must you begin?

C_____ the C_____

If you are willing to continue in the process of submitting to God, who alone decides right and wrong, conclude today's study in prayer, using the following as a guide:

Father God, I praise you because _____.
I want to _____.
I ask you to _____.
Help me to _____.
   In Jesus' name. Amen.

Dear Diary

Monica said good night to her mother and closed her bedroom door. She reached into the drawer of her nightstand, pulled out her diary, and began to write.

Saw Jimmy in line at the movies today. He was talking to Susan Brock. He was with friends and she was with her parents.

I can't wait to see Gina tomorrow. I'll smile like we're still friends and tell her that I saw the two of them in line together at the movies. I'll tell her how pretty Susan looked and how close they were standing. That ought to give Gina something to think about. With any luck, she'll throw one of her temper tantrums around Jimmy. He'll finally see what she's _really_ like. Maybe they'll even get mad and break up.

The best part is, I'll only be telling the truth. I won't be doing a thing wrong. Just teaching my former best friend a lesson.

Monica is still trying to judge the rightness or wrongness of her actions herself. If she would consider her action as a choice between what is right or wrong objectively, she could proceed to the next step in making right choices, which is to:

Compare it to God.

C_____ it to G_____.

The Second C

What would happen if Monica compared her action to the nature and character of God? What would she learn by tracing her choice (through precept and principle) to the Person of God Himself?

Precept

Do you remember Jesus' words in the introduction to this week's study? Read *Matthew 22:34-40.* How do His words apply to Monica's situation?

_____

_____

_____

_____

_____

_____

Read *Matthew 5:43-46.* What precept did Jesus quote? _____

_____

_____

What precept did Jesus issue? _____

_____

How do you think those verses apply to Monica's situation? _____

_____

_____

_____

_____

Principle

What positive principle do you think lies behind each of those precepts? (Hint: It is the principle that Jesus said all the commandments express in one way or another.)

_____

Person

What is it, then, about God that the precepts and the principle point to? Is there something in God's nature and character that would make Monica's action toward Gina wrong?

Read the following Bible verses and complete the statement that follows.

1 John 4:8   God is _____

1 John 4:16   God is _____

2 Corinthians 13:11   God is "the God of _____"

If Monica were trying to judge right and wrong according to the 4Cs (instead of justifying it according to her emotions), she would be able to see that her action would be wrong. Regardless of how Gina treated her, regardless of how much she misses Jimmy, regardless of whether she could accomplish it without (technically) lying, her action would be wrong. If you compare it to God, you will discover that her action would be wrong because:

- God's precepts command us to love.
- God's precepts command us to love because God values love.
- God values love because God is love.

Monica's attitude and action toward Gina is wrong because it is not loving. It contradicts the nature of God, who is love.

Monica and You

Are there any unloving attitudes in your heart and mind? Are you contemplating or pursuing any actions that are contradictory to His nature and character (as revealed through precept-principle-person)?

List below any attitudes that you need to submit to God's standard of love:

my attitude toward _____

my attitude about _____

_____

_____

_____

List below any actions that you need to change, based on God's standard of love:

the way I act toward _____

the way I act when _____

_____

_____

_____

Close today's study with a prayer asking God to reveal to you any actions or attitudes you need to compare to Him.

Monica's Obstacle

Monica sat up on the edge of her bed. She cast a glance at the red numbers of her lighted clock. It was 12:10 a.m.

She had been tossing and turning in bed since 10 o'clock and had not slept at all. She had been thinking about tomorrow, about her plans for Gina, and about Jimmy.

Something was bothering her about all this. She turned on the light beside her bed and stared at the poster-covered walls for a few moments. Then she turned her gaze upon her desk, where her schoolbooks were stacked next to her Bible and her *Right Choices* Workbook.

This is too weird, she thought. *I feel like I'm one of those kids in that Workbook.* She and her church youth group had been working through the book, learning how to discern right from wrong and how to make right choices.

"This is different, though," she said, feeling as if she were talking not only to herself, but to Someone else as well. "I mean, I know God said we should love each other, and that love is a big thing to Him because He is love and all that, but this is different."

She frowned. "I mean, Jimmy was my boyfriend first. Gina had no right to do what she did." She stood for a moment, then plopped back down onto the edge of her bed. "It was wrong for her to do what she did, not for me to do what I'm going to do."

She turned out the light and laid back down on her bed. She closed her eyes, and waited for sleep to come.

Wait a minute! What's going on? It seems like Monica has considered the choice and even compared it to God. . . yet she's still determined to carry out her plan.

Yup. That's because the first two steps toward making right choices require an admission of God's sovereignty; the third step demands submission. And that's where Monica's having trouble. She doesn't want to turn from her own selfish ways, so she is finding ways to justify her actions according to her individual situation instead of submitting and committing to God's ways.

Ancient People, Modern Problem

Turn to *1 Samuel 26,* the story of Saul and David in the Desert of Ziph. Read *verses 1-8.*

Had Saul ever mistreated David? If so, how? _____

_____

Read *verses 9-13*. How did David respond to Saul's mistreatment? ____

_____

Read *verses 14-25*. Why do you think David responded that way?_____

_____

Read *2 Samuel 1:1-4,17-24*. How did David respond when he heard of Saul's death?

_____

_____

Read *2 Samuel 2:1-7*. How does David's action in these passages compare with God? How does it compare with Monica's action?

_____

_____

_____

_____

Your Mission

What do you think Monica should do? (check all that apply)

❑ Go ahead with the plan to tell Gina about Jimmy and Susan at the movies.
❑ Ask her Mom for advice.
❑ Ask your Mom for advice.
❑ Commit to God's way.
❑ Get a friend to tell Gina about Jimmy and Susan at the movies.
❑ Figure some other way to get even with Gina.
❑ Give up on ever going out with Jimmy.
❑ Resolve to do the right thing no matter what.
❑ Forget the plan but pray that Gina gets what she deserves.
❑ Find ways to show God's love to Gina and Jimmy.
❑ Find ways to show a quick uppercut to Gina's chin and a short left jab to her nose.

Do you think committing to God's way would be easy for Monica?

❑ Yes   ❑ No

What do you think would be hardest for her? _____

What is hardest for you about committing to God's way? _____

_____

_____

_____

Commit to God's ways.

Once you commit to God's way, remember: you need to depend on Him to give you the power to walk in His ways. None of us can consistently make right choices on our own; we need His help.

Have you committed to His ways? Are you depending on His help? Close today's study with a prayer renewing your commitment and thanking God for giving you the power to walk in His ways.

Choose Your Own Adventure

Have you ever read a "Choose Your Own Adventure" book? It's a type of book that occasionally allows the reader to choose which action the character should take. "If Howard stays to confront the big hairy beast," the book might say, "turn to page 34. If Howard escapes through the tunnel, turn to page 46."

If you could choose your own adventure for Monica, how would you make it end? Put the finishing touches on Monica's story by filling in the blanks according to what choice you think she would make, and the benefits or consequences that might result.

Monica rolled out of bed the next morning and rubbed the sleep out of her eyes.

"I've made my decision," she told herself, sounding more determined than she felt. "I'm going to _____."

She rushed through breakfast and arrived at school in time to see Gina standing at her locker near the chemistry lab. She eyed her former friend carefully, looking up and down the hall for any sign of Jimmy. The coast was clear.

"Hi, Gina," she said sweetly. Gina's eyes widened at Monica's greeting. "I've got something I need to tell you. _____
_____
What do you think about that?"

Gina's eyes clouded with tears. She couldn't believe what she was hearing.

"I'll see you later, okay?" Monica said, inwardly congratulating herself for the effect her words had obviously had on Gina. She turned and walked down the hall, nearly skipping with self-satisfaction.

She thought about what she had done for the rest of the day. It made her feel _____, knowing that she had _____
_____. Somehow, in her heart, she knew
_____ and from now
on, _____
_____
_____.

Count On It

The last of the 4Cs, you'll remember, is to **count on God's protection and provision.** According to the story you wrote, will Monica be able to count on God's protection and provision?

She may not instantly realize many of the benefits of making the right choice, but if she commits to God's way and then begins to thank Him for His loving protection and provision—even if she never sees any benefits—she will pave the way for a much happier and healthier future.

Count on God's protection and provision.

Why? Because **God's standard of love protects from strife and provides for peace.** Have you ever seen a willful two-year-old express his anger by biting *himself?* Such behavior illustrates the fact that hatred and hostility harms us more than anyone at whom we may aim our hatred. God knows that unloving attitudes and actions poison our own lives, and fill them with strife; a life of love toward others is a life of peace.

God's standard of love protects from self-centeredness and provides for fulfillment. Perhaps you know someone who evaluates every conversation, every relationship, every event of life in terms of how it will personally affect them. Such a person may have some friends and acquaintances without really loving any of them. The person who loves God and others expresses interest in the ideas and pursuits of others, often enjoys giving as much as receiving, and finds joy in sharing with others and caring for them. Such a person naturally tends to be more appreciated and successful than the self-centered individual.

God's standard of love protects from spiritual barrenness and provides for spiritual blessing. John the apostle wrote, *Anyone who does not love remains in death. Anyone who hates his brother is a murderer, and you know that no murderer has eternal life in him (1 John 3:14b-15).* Such strong language communicates the tragic spiritual consequences God wants to protect us from; that is why He commands us to love. He wants to protect us from the barrenness of an unloving soul and provide the spiritual blessings that spring from *the most excellent way (1 Cor. 12:31)* of love.

These are not the only ways that obedience to God's command to love Him and others protects us and provides for us. Can you think of any others?

• God's standard of love protects from _____ and provides for _____.

• God's standard of love protects from _____ and provides for _____.

• God's standard of love protects from _____ and provides for _____.

The King and I

Let's learn once more about David's confrontation with Saul, the first king of Israel. Read *1 Samuel 26:21-25.* Copy or paraphrase the words of David that reveal that he was counting on God's protection and provision:

_____

_____

_____

_____

_____

_____

_____

According to the biblical record (in *1 Sam. 26:1-25*), do you think David (check all that apply):

❏ considered the choice
❏ compared it to God
❏ committed to God's way
❏ counted on God's protection and provision

In which of the 4Cs are you having the most success yourself?

_____

_____

_____

_____

Conclude today's study by spending some time in prayer, thanking God for your success in that area and confiding in Him about your struggles in other areas.

4Cs

week 6

The Land of Magoo

T he famous explorer raised his mighty machete over his shoulder and swung it hard, slicing through the thick jungle growth that blocked his way.

He and his native guide stepped through the opening he had made and gazed in wonder at the legendary land of Magoo.

"Look now," the guide said, "before the magic of Magoo blurs your sight."

The explorer stared, wide-eyed, at the scene before him. He watched as a man walked down the sidewalk of a tiny village and collided head-on with a sign that bore the message, "Caution: Sign blocking sidewalk." A woman opened the front door of her home and waved a cheerful greeting to a nearby telephone pole. A young girl, her arms filled with school books, entered a delicatessen, sat in a chair, opened her notebook, and began copying the delicatessen menu on the blackboard.

"It is as you say, then," the explorer muttered in amazement. "The people of Magoo cannot tell a pole from a person or a delicatessen from a school."

The guide nodded. "Their sight is blurred by the magic of Magoo. They do not know night from day or right from left." He realized that he was squinting to see the village below. "We must go. The magic will soon cloud our eyes."

"I can see just fine," the explorer retorted. He turned his gaze on his guide, whose hazy form seemed to be enshrouded in fog. "I want to know more of this magical land." He began walking down the slope toward Magoo.

The guide shook his head and turned back into the jungle. He had seen it before; the land of Magoo did strange things to people.

The land of Magoo is mythical, of course, but what happens to visitors to Magoo seems to happen in real life to people who must decide between right and wrong in matters pertaining to love and sex.

People in love—including high-school and junior-high-school-age kids—seem to enter a magical place or dimension that blurs their sight and clouds their perception of right and wrong. Men and women who possess strong biblical values in other areas often exhibit a strange fogginess about right and wrong when it comes to love and sex.

But you will see, as a result of this week's studies, that the **4Cs** method for making right choices provides valuable insight into questions you have, or will have soon, about romantic love and sex.

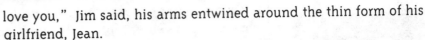

Jim and Jean

love you," Jim said, his arms entwined around the thin form of his girlfriend, Jean.

"I love you, too," she answered. She leaned backward and soon they were lying together on the couch in Jean's living room.

Jim and Jean had been dating since their sophomore year in high school and had even begun talking about marriage. They were both Christians, but their relationship had lately become more intense than ever, and it seemed nearly impossible now to continue to postpone the inevitable.

"When are your parents supposed to come home?" Jim asked.

"Late," she answered, understanding the reason for Jim's question. She and Jim loved each other, and she was sure this was the boy she would marry.

Their kisses became more passionate, and they began to do things they had never done before in several years of dating. Neither of them said anything, but both understood they wouldn't "go all the way." They both intended to save that for their wedding night. In fact, that was one of the reasons Jean loved him, because he wanted to be a virgin when he got married.

But tonight, each of them reasoned, there was no longer any reason to hold back. What difference could it possibly make? It would be wrong if they didn't love each other, of course. It would be wrong if they weren't serious. It would be wrong to actually have intercourse. But surely, Jim and Jean figured, what they were doing wasn't wrong. Not for them. Not under the circumstances.

"I love you," Jean murmured in Jim's ear.

"I love you, too," he answered.

It Feels So Right

Jim and Jean are in a difficult situation, and their struggle is intensified by emotional and chemical factors. They must contend not only with the intellectual and spiritual issues, but with their passions—and their raging hormones.

Those are some of the things that make choices in the area of love and sex so difficult. Like the magic of Magoo, such powerful emotional and chemical forces can blur your vision and make it even harder for guys and girls in love to see—and choose—right from wrong.

A huge hit song some years ago contained the line, "It can't be wrong, 'cause it feels so right." That kind of thinking is common among people in love, but it overlooks an important truth: feelings don't determine what's right or wrong.

Think back to week one and two; based on your discoveries in those studies, what does determine what's right or wrong? _____

This Week's Verse—

You were bought at a price. Therefore honor God with your body.
1 Corinthians 6:20

_____

_____

_____

_____

_____

_____

_____

_____

Look back on Jim and Jean's story on page 104; circle or highlight words or phrases that refer to their thought processes; then, using the chart below, draw a bar graph to reflect what you think are the main factors influencing Jim and Jean's decision:

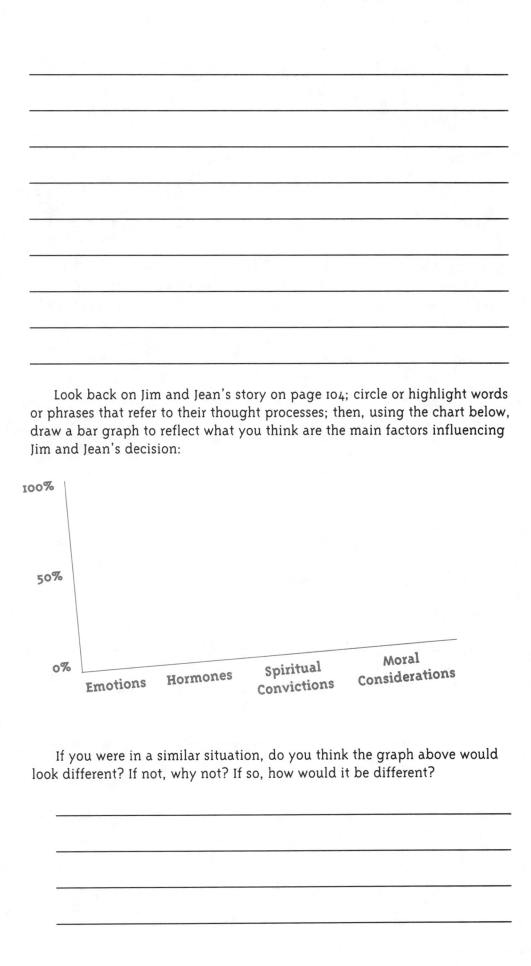

If you were in a similar situation, do you think the graph above would look different? If not, why not? If so, how would it be different?

_____

_____

_____

_____

Why would it be different?_____

_____

_____

_____

_____

Chapter and Verse

Jim and Jean are Christians, and they usually have no trouble figuring right from wrong; they just figure that things are different for them than for most couples.

Are they right? Can you think of any Bible verses or passages that might apply to their situation? (If you have a study Bible or a Bible with a concordance, use the concordance or topical index to help you answer.) If so, what are they?

_____

_____

_____

_____

_____

Can you think of any biblical concepts or principles that might apply? If so, what are they?

_____

_____

_____

_____

_____

Do you have an easier time figuring out what's right or wrong for Jim and Jean than you do figuring out what's right or wrong for yourself?

❑ Yes   ❑ No

If yes, why do you think that's the case? _____

_____

_____

_____

_____

Do you find it easier to *discern* what's right or to do what's right?

_____

_____

_____

Why do you think that's the case?_____

_____

_____

_____

_____

Close today's study with a prayer, first praising God for who He is, then thanking Him for what He does, and finally asking God to help you to both discern and do what is right as you submit yourself to Him and commit yourself to His ways.

Passion's Power

day 2

Jean closed her eyes as she returned Jim's passionate kiss. Her heart felt as though it were beating a thousand times a minute, and she felt suddenly out of breath.

She and Jim struggled against the crowded confines of the couch and the constraints of their clothing.

"Ow!" she said, as Jim's elbow pinned her hair to the couch cushion.

"I'm sorry," he cooed. "Are you all right?"

"Yes," she answered. "Just move your elbow."

He shifted his weight and then closed his eyes and leaned into her again to kiss her. She did not close her eyes, but cast a wary eye at the clock on the mantel; she didn't want to lose track of time. Her parents could return home as early as midnight.

Jim and Jean have resisted the temptation to engage in premarital sex or heavy petting for several years now, yet they are giving in to their passions now. Why? List the things below that you think have prompted their decision to become more physically involved:

_____

_____

_____

_____

_____

Do you think Jim and Jean expect to enjoy some immediate benefits as a result of their decision? What would such benefits be?

_____

_____

_____

_____

Do those things make their behavior right?

❏ Yes, because_____

_____

❑ No, because_____

_____

You see, they are trying to judge right and wrong (which is objective) by their passions (which are subjective). They are letting their raging hormones cloud their judgment of right and wrong.

What should they do rather than justifying their actions and proclaiming them "right" because of their plans and passions?

C_____ the C_____

Considering the choice means remembering that their choice is not

between _____, but between

_____, regardless of what they think.

Consider the choice.

A King-Sized Bed

Second Samuel 11 contains the story of David, and a horribly wrong choice he made.

Read *2 Samuel 11:1-17, 26-27.*

Do you think David's choice was right or wrong? _____

Why do you say that? _____

_____

_____

Do you think David might have tried to justify his choice to become physically involved with Bathsheba? What kinds of reasons could he have given to make his conduct seem "right?"

_____

_____

David and Bathsheba

Do you think David tried to judge right and wrong (which is objective) by his passions (which were subjective)?

❑ Yes   ❑ No

Does the scriptural account give any indication that David **considered the choice?**

❏ Yes   ❏ No

Do you think he **considered the choice** as a choice between what was objectively right and what was objectively wrong, regardless of what he thought or felt?

❏ Yes   ❏ No

Look Inside

What about you? Do you ever try to judge right and wrong by your passions? If so, what can you do today to **consider the choice,** to start making your choices based on a belief in an objective, universal, constant standard of right and wrong?

_____

_____

_____

_____

_____

_____

Spend a few moments in prayer, using the following as a guideline:

- Praise God because He is righteous, loving, holy, and true.

- Talk to God honestly about the changes you would like to make in the way you make choices.

- Ask Him to give you patience and perseverance as you continue in this study.

- Pray for your family and friends, asking God to use you to bless them.

Clearing the Fog

day 3

Asleepy Jean wrestled into her Sunday clothes and shuffled back into the bathroom. The mirror was still fogged from the hot shower she had taken a few moments before.

She snatched a hand towel from the rack and wiped the mirror with it, clearing a space large enough for her to put her contact lenses in her still-sleepy eyes.

Jim left a little before midnight last night. Their passion had carried them further than ever before, but they had stayed true to their determination not to go "all the way."

Jean looked unsmilingly at her reflection. "I don't feel guilty," she whispered, as if trying to convince herself. "Why should I? I love him and he loves me, that's all that matters."

She stared at herself, unmoving. The mirror began to fog again, and she reached for the towel.

The bathroom mirror isn't the only thing that keeps fogging up for Jean; her thinking isn't too clear, either, because she's trying to judge the rightness or wrongness of her actions herself. She's not considering the choice as a choice between what is right or wrong objectively (regardless of what she thinks). Consequently, she's not proceeding to the next step in the 4C process, which is: _____

_____

Dare to Compare

Realistically, Jean may be reluctant to submit her decision to the 4C process because she doesn't want to compare her actions to the nature and character of God; she may be afraid of what she'll discover.

What would she discover if she were to **compare it** (her action) **to God?** What would she learn by tracing her action (through precept and principle) to the Person of God Himself?

Compare it to God.

Precept

In biblical terms, sexual immorality is all extramarital (including premarital) sex. God has spoken through the law, and He has made His standard clear: all sexual involvement outside of marriage is wrong.

Copy the precept as it is expressed in the following verses:

_____ (*Acts 15:29*).

_____ (*1 Cor. 6:18*).

_____ (1 Cor. 10:8).

_____ (Eph. 5:3).

_____ (Col. 3:5).

_____ (1 Thess. 4:3).

Do you think the above precepts apply to Jim and Jean's situation?

❑ Yes, because _____

❑ No, because _____

Principle

What positive principle or principles do you think lie behind those precepts?

_____

Hebrews 13:4—
Marriage should be
honored by all,
and the marriage
bed kept pure, for
God will judge the
adulterer and all the
sexually immoral.

The biblical commands to "flee sexual immorality" are based on God's standards for sex, which actually incorporate *three* principles: love, purity, and faithfulness.

According to the Bible *(Rom. 13:9-10; Eph. 5:28)*, true love is evident when the happiness, health, and spiritual growth of another person is as important to you as your own.

God's standard for sex is one of purity. Copy *Hebrews 13:4* here: _____

_____

_____

_____

_____

He designed sex to be enjoyed in a husband-wife relationship, for procreation *(Gen. 1:28)*, for spiritual unity *(Gen. 2:24)*, and for recreation *(Prov. 5:18-19)*. It's meant to form an unbroken circle, a pure union: two virgins entering an exclusive relationship. That circle, that union, can be broken even *before* marriage, if one or both of the partners has not kept the marriage bed pure by waiting to have sex until it can be done in the purity of a husband-wife relationship.

God's standard for sex is also one of faithfulness. Love *always protects, always trusts, always hopes, always perseveres (I Cor. 13:7). Love and faithfulness meet together,* the Bible says *(Ps. 85:10)*. In practical terms, this means that love, true love, requires a commitment of two people to remain faithful to each other. That is why marriage is central to biblical sexuality, because it binds two people together in a lifelong commitment. If love is to produce the emotional, physical, and spiritual intimacy it is designed to produce, it must be committed, faithful love. Jim and Jean may be talking about marriage, they might even get engaged, but until they are husband and wife, they have not fully committed to each other and fulfilled God's requirement for sex.

God's precepts regarding human sexuality are grounded upon the principles of love, purity, and faithfulness. Those principles, in turn, reflect the person of God Himself.

Person

Those principles are right because they are from God—they reflect His nature and character. Read the following Bible verses and complete the statement that follows:

I John 4:8   God is _____

I John 3:3   He (God) is _____

Deuteronomy 7:9   He (God) is the _____ God.

If Jim and Jean compare their actions to the nature and character of God (instead of justifying it by their passions), how do you think they would answer the following?

T   F   Their action is loving; it promotes the happiness, health, and spiritual growth of the other person.

T   F   Their action is pure; it does not defile the marriage bed by permitting activity that should be reserved for a husband or wife.

T   F   Their action is faithful; both partners have made a lifetime commitment of marriage.

Shine the Light

Because God is pure, sexual impurity is an offense against Him. Because He is faithful, sex outside of a marriage commitment is an affront to Him. King David, who sinned with Bathsheba, later repented; he confessed to God, *Against you, you only, have I sinned and done what is evil in your sight (Ps. 51:4).* Was David ignoring the fact that his sin had affected other people, resulting in the death of Bathsheba's husband, Uriah, and of the baby Bathsheba bore David? No, he was acknowledging the fundamental fact that when he sinned with Bathsheba, he sinned against the Lawgiver. His act was wrong because it offended God's standard for sex: love, purity, and faithfulness.

David realized his sin was against God.

Do your relationships conform to that standard? Are you tolerating any wrong attitudes or actions in this area? If so, turn to David's prayer in *Psalm 51,* and read *verses 1-12,* making them your prayer.

Close your study time today by asking God to give you loving, faithful, and pure relationships that honor Him and your future husband or wife.

On Bended Knee

J im sat in the choir loft at church, his choir folder open on his lap. The choir director lifted her arms as the pastor concluded his sermon.

Jim opened his mouth to sing, but nothing came out; instead, he watched with wide-eyed interest as Jean rose from her seat in the congregation and walked forward to kneel at the front of the sanctuary.

He watched his girlfriend, thoughts racing through his head like hockey players skating back and forth in a hockey rink.

What's she doing? he wondered. *I hope she's not having second thoughts about last night. I hope she's not feeling guilty, like we did something wrong.*

He stared at her intensely, as if he could transmit his will to her by sheer will power.

Don't let it bother you, Jean. We're too much in love.

The choir sang all around Jim, but he never even looked in the choir director's direction.

You've got nothing to repent for, he told Jean, who still knelt alone. *Don't ruin it all now. Don't ruin it all.*

Jim is in trouble. He has not entirely convinced himself that his activity with Jean is perfectly okay. He senses that, if he did consider the choice and compare it to God, he and Jean would have to admit the wrongness of their actions. So, he's stubbornly trying to ignore what his heart and mind know: that he should turn from his own selfish ways and commit to God's way.

Better Late Than Never

Jim's not the first to make that mistake (chances are, you've done the same thing yourself).

Remember King David and his incredibly bad choices with Bathsheba? You probably know that the story didn't end after David engineered the death of Uriah, Bathsheba's husband.

Read *2 Samuel 12:1-13.* How did David finally come to admit the wrongness of his actions? _____

_____

Do you think *verse 13* reflects a sudden realization or do you think David sensed his sinfulness all along? Why or why not? _____

_____

_____

Do you think *verse 13* corresponds with any of the **4Cs**? If so, which one?

_____

_____

_____

Read *Psalm 51:1-17*, the song David composed after the prophet Nathan confronted him with his sin. Based on these verses, do you think David committed to God's way?

❏ Yes   ❏ No

Why or why not? _____

Better Safe Than Sorry

How is David's situation similar to Jim and Jean's?_____

_____

_____

_____

How is it different? _____

_____

_____

What do you think committing to God's way would involve for Jim? (check all that apply)

- ❏ break up with Jean
- ❏ keep his mouth shut and see what happens
- ❏ admit his sexual sin to God
- ❏ marry Jean immediately
- ❏ join the circus
- ❏ determine to save all forms of sexual intimacy for marriage
- ❏ "go all the way" with Jean
- ❏ resolve to build a relationship that reflects love, purity, and faithfulness
- ❏ become a monk
- ❏ avoid being alone with Jean in dark or secluded places
- ❏ avoid being alone with anybody in dark or secluded places
- ❏ avoid dark or secluded places

Committing to God's way always means that we have to make a change in our actions.

Do you think committing to God's way would be easy for Jim?

❏ Yes   ❏ No

What do you think would be hardest for him? _____

_____

_____

What is hardest for you about committing to God's way in this area?

_____

_____

How can you give that problem to God? _____

_____

Close today's study by writing your own "Psalm 51" below in which you admit God's sovereignty, submit to His version of what's right or wrong, and commit to following His ways in the power of His Holy Spirit.

_____

_____

_____

_____

_____

_____

_____

_____

_____

_____

_____

Change of Heart

Jim gripped Jean by the elbow and pulled her aside in the church foyer.

"Are you okay?" he asked, his eyes searching her face for clues as to why she had knelt in the front of the sanctuary at the end of the morning service.

"Yeah," she nodded, avoiding his gaze. "We need to talk."

Jim didn't like the sound of that. "Walk you out to the parking lot?"

She nodded. She folded her arms across her chest, and they walked in silence to a corner of the church parking lot and paused by a sprawling six-foot juniper bush.

"What's up?" he asked, fearing he already knew the answer.

She looked into Jim's brown eyes and swallowed hard. Then she dropped her gaze to the ground. "I prayed about last night," she whispered. "I told God I knew it was wrong, and I told Him I'd try not to do it again."

"What did we do?" Jim asked, his voice rising suddenly in pitch. "We didn't do anything!"

She didn't answer, but her expression clearly communicated that she knew better.

"Look," Jim said, consciously controlling his voice, "I love you. And I thought you loved me."

"I do."

"If this is about getting engaged. . . "

"No," she answered calmly. "It's not. It's about doing what's right." He started to interrupt, but she wouldn't let him. "Not what you say is right, and not what I say is right. It's about what God says."

"So," Jim said slowly, pausing between words. "What about us? We're still a couple, right?"

She looked at him without blinking. "I don't know," she said. "I don't know."

Can You Count?

Do you think Jean made the right decision? Or is she making a big mistake? What were the immediate results of her choice? List them below:

_____

_____

_____

Do you think the results are immediately positive or negative? _____

Count on God's protection and provision.

The last of the 4Cs, you'll remember, is to **count on God's protection and provision.** What kinds of protection and provision do you think could result from Jean's decision to commit to God's way? _____

_____

Whether those potential benefits are the reason she made her decision or whether she's obeying God in faith, and simply trusting Him with the results, she is paving the way for a much happier, healthier future.

Why? Because. . .

God's standards for sexual behavior protect from guilt.— Because God defines right and wrong, when we transgress His standards, we will invariably suffer guilt. Jean and Jim's repeated assertions that they had no reason to feel guilty should have tipped them off; they felt it necessary to convince themselves because they did feel guilty. . . as will anyone who does wrong.

God's standards for sexual behavior provide for spiritual rewards.— The blessing of a clear conscience and an unhindered walk with God are inestimable. It is an immeasurable blessing to be able to stand before an altar and proclaim the singular devotion of your body to your mate and to God. The sexual relationship between a husband and wife is not only pleasurable, it is sacred.

God's standards for sexual behavior protect from unplanned pregnancies and abortions.— Every day in America, 2,795 teenage girls get pregnant and 1,106 have an abortion. Those girls who carry their babies for the full term often face overwhelming difficulties; many drop out of school, many experience physical problems, many feel left out of "normal" teen activities because of their responsibility to a child. Those girls who abort their children are not delivered from such consequences; abortion produces traumatic results, too. Over half report preoccupation with the aborted child, flashbacks of the abortion experience, and nightmares related to the abortion.[1]

God's standards for sexual behavior protect from sexually transmitted diseases.— Every day in America, 4,219 teenagers contract a sexually transmitted disease. Yet not one of those incidents has occurred between two mutually faithful partners who entered the relationship sexually pure. . . because God's standards for sexual behavior protect from sexually transmitted diseases.

God's standards for sexual behavior provide for peace of mind.— Two people who adhere to God's wise model will enjoy a relationship free of fear, free of disease, free of the "ghosts" of past partners, and free of "emotional baggage" as a result of a past immoral relationship.

God's standards for sexual behavior provide for trust.— Sexual purity and faithfulness before marriage contributes to an atmosphere of trust within marriage. That trust provides peace of mind for both partners when they are apart; each knows that the other is worthy of trust. Why? Because, in the period before their marriage, they proved their character, their maturity, and their self-control.

God's rewards are always best for us in every situation.

God's standards for sexual behavior provide for true intimacy.—
God's standard for sexual behavior produces a degree of intimacy that only exists in the committed exclusivity of a marriage relationship. *For this reason,* God said, *a man will leave his father and mother and be united to his wife, and they will become one flesh (Gen. 2:24).*

God's design for sexual intimacy protects from many dangers, and provides the best climate for the enjoyment of spiritual rewards, peace of mind, trust, intimacy, and many other benefits, to be enjoyed in a lifelong relationship of purity and faithfulness.

Costly Choice

The story of David and Bathsheba graphically depicts the results of David's refusal to follow God's way. Read *2 Samuel 12:13-25* and answer the following multiple choice questions (circle the correct choice):

1. As a result of David's choice, Bathsheba became:
   (a) pregnant
   (b) David's wife
   (c) a widow
   (d) all of the above
2. As a result of David's choice, God:
   (a) stopped loving David
   (b) rewarded David
   (c) was displeased with David
   (d) struck David with leprosy
3. As a result of David's choice, the baby:
   (a) grew up to be king
   (b) became a great warrior
   (c) brought years of joy to his parents
   (d) none of the above
4. As a result of David's choice, David:
   (a) brought shame on the name of the Lord
   (b) lost his firstborn son
   (c) spent seven days in agony and uncertainty
   (d) all of the above

Answers: 1- (d); 2- (c); 3- (d); 4- (d)

Looking back on his sin with Bathsheba, do you think David experienced immediate benefits as a result of his decision?

❑ Yes   ❑ No

Do you think the consequences were worth the immediate benefits?

❑ Yes   ❑ No

Why or why not? _____

_____

For thought: Do your choices in this area reflect a desire to get immediate benefits (like David) or a willingness to obey God and count on his long-term protection and provision (like Jean)?

Close today's study in prayer, using the following as a guide:

Father, I praise You because You are a loving and righteous God. Thank You for Your desire to protect me and provide for me. I sincerely want to please You and enjoy the blessings of following Your ways. As I face important choices, help me to:
Consider the choice,
Compare it to You,
Commit to Your way, and then
Count on Your protection and provision.
I trust You to help me do that, every day, by Your Holy Spirit, in Jesus' name. Amen.

[1]Anne Catherine Speckhard, "Psycho-Social Aspects of Stress Following Abortion," (doctoral dissertation, University of Minnesota, 1985), n.p.

week 7

week

weekseven

week

Two-Minute Warning

He turned in time to see the two gigantic creatures who were poised to pounce on him, but not in time to avoid them. In a blinding, crunching flash, Tony Ortiz was pinned to the ground in a flurry of sweat, muscle, and dirt.

"Hi ya, Tony," one of the animals said as he crushed Tony's form beneath his 235 pounds. The big lineman stood up and offered a helping hand to the quarterback he had just sacked.

Tony stood and suddenly heard a sound like a gun being fired. He looked at the other players; they were all walking off the field.

Tony pumped the air with his fists and danced to the sidelines.

"We did it, Coach!" he yelled. He jumped up and down like a ballerina in front of Coach Burns. "We won!"

Coach Burns opened his mouth to say something, but Tony was shouting excitedly, slapping his teammates on their backs and cheering their season-ending championship effort. Finally, the coach gripped Tony by the face mask and pulled his helmeted head until coach and player were nearly touching noses.

"Tony!" he bellowed. "Get a grip, man! We haven't won yet."

"Huh?" Tony asked, contorting his face into a picture of confusion.

"That was the two-minute warning, Tony," the coach said. "We still have two minutes to play."

Tony looked up at the game clock on the scoreboard. It registered a two followed by two zeros. He turned to face Coach Burns again.

"Oh," he said. He flashed a sheepish smile like a cartoon character who's just discovered a lighted stick of dynamite in his pocket.

You may smile at Tony's mistake. But it's an easy mistake to make. In fact, right now you may be in danger of doing much the same thing.

For the past six weeks, you've been on a journey of discovery, learning how to make good choices in a world that's gone bad. You've applied the 4C process for making right choices to various issues, such as honesty, love, and sex. You've searched the Scriptures, and come to understand that the line between right and wrong is a reflection of God's nature and character; what is like Him is right, and what is unlike Him is wrong.

Today you begin the last week of study in your *Right Choices* Workbook. If you've worked diligently through the past six weeks of studies and participated in the youth group sessions, you may have a pretty good understanding of absolute truth, how to discern it, and how to follow it.

But you're not finished yet. Because this week's studies will tackle some important issues—things you're sure to come up against as you begin to apply the truth to your life.

To borrow a term from football, you might say this is the two-minute warning. That means the game's not over. This is no time to let up; if anything, it's time to play with more intensity and determination than before.

Pshaw's Point

So, anyway, you're sitting in your fourth-period class the day before summer vacation starts, writing a note to Jennifer, who sits two rows over, and you're suddenly aware that the teacher, Mr. Pshaw, has called your name two or three times.

"Uh," you answer fluently, "Huh? Wha?"

"I was asking," Mr. Pshaw says in his whiny, don't-you-think-I-have-better-things-to-do-than-try-to-teach-the-mysteries-of-the-universe-to-unappreciative-adolescents-like-yourself voice, "what you will be doing with the knowledge you have gained in this course."

"Oh," you answer. You panic for a moment, unable to remember exactly what course he's been teaching you for the last few months. Then, in a flash of inspiration, you remember, and blurt the answer out loud. "Earth Science."

Mr. Pshaw looks at you like you've just sprouted a second head. "That is correct," he says, addressing you by your full name. "You are in Earth Science at the moment."

Titters of laughter break out among the other students in the room. You suddenly wish you'd agreed to go on the church mission trip to Madagascar that left two days ago.

"But that's not what I asked," Mr. Pshaw continues. "I would like to know what you plan to do with the knowledge you have gained in this course."

"Oh, yeah. Right," you say, still searching your mind for the suggestion of an answer. *This is Earth Science, for crying out loud,* you complain to yourself. *What am I supposed to say, "I plan to open a waste treatment plant in my backyard?"* Instead, you decide to stall for time. "Well, Mr. Pshaw," you say. "It's really hard to say. I mean, we've learned so much in this class, it'll probably take a long time before we realize all the ways it applies to our lives."

The titters begin again, but you swallow hard and face Mr. Pshaw without smiling. His eyebrows crease together and he looks at you suspiciously.

"Yes," he says, clearing his throat. "Well, that's true." He rubs his fingers under his chin as he studies you long and hard. Finally, he turns and points to another student. You breathe a sigh of relief as he asks Gary Belcher, "What will you do the next time the bagger at the grocery store asks, 'Paper or plastic?'"

Now What?

Of course, the day before school lets out for the summer, you're not likely to be planning what to do with the knowledge you gained in the past school year. But Mr. Pshaw did have a decent point.

After all, many of us want to know, when we take a class, that the knowledge we gain is going to be useful. . . at least sometime, somewhere.

This Week's Verse—

For our struggle is not against flesh and blood, but against the rulers, against the authorities, against the powers of this dark world and against the spiritual forces of evil in the heavenly realms.
Ephesians 6:12

We wouldn't sign up for swim class if we never expected to go swimming again. Most of us wouldn't take a course in painting trash can lids if we didn't expect it to come in handy someday, right? And what's the use of Earth Science if we never use the knowledge we gain? (Okay, okay, except that it does count as a science credit, which some of us need desperately in order to graduate before the year 3000.)

So what's the use of a course in truth? What can you expect to gain from a study called *Right Choices?* And how are you going to put that knowledge to work in the weeks and months after you finish the course?

Setting You Free

In *John 8:31-32*, Jesus spoke some important words—words that deal with Pshaw's point. Copy those verses on the lines below (you'll be referring to them throughout the rest of this study):

_____

_____

_____

_____

_____

_____

What did Jesus say would mark a person as His disciple? "If you _____

_____."

Which of the **4Cs** do you think that refers to?_____

What did Jesus say would be the result of "holding to [His] teaching?" (circle one)

> (a) Then you will earn eternal life
> (b) Then you will know the truth
> (c) Then you will gain rewards in heaven
> (d) Then you will learn how to paint trash can lids

Notice that Jesus said, *"If you hold to my teaching. . . .Then you will know the truth."* Think about that for a moment. Why do you think He said it that way, instead of, "If you know the truth, then you will hold to My teaching?"

_____

_____

_____

What did Jesus say would be the benefit of knowing the truth?

_____

_____

_____

_____

What do you think Jesus meant by that? *How* can the truth set you free? (check all that apply):

- ❏ by letting you do whatever you want
- ❏ by giving you the ability to tell right from wrong and good choices from bad
- ❏ by making it so you don't have to listen to your parents anymore
- ❏ by freeing you from the consequences of wrong choices
- ❏ by giving you a doctor's excuse so you don't have to climb ropes in gym
- ❏ by giving you confidence to stand up for what you believe
- ❏ by enabling you to more intelligently explain the truth to your friends
- ❏ by opening your eyes to the loving motivation behind God's commands
- ❏ by releasing you from uncertainty about which choices are best in certain situations
- ❏ by empowering you to fulfill God's best plans and your highest potential

How would you answer if Mr. Pshaw asked you his question about this *Right Choices* study? What do you plan to do with the knowledge you have gained in this course?

_____

_____

_____

That's what this week's Workbook studies are about. You've learned an awful lot about the truth: Who determines it, how to recognize it, and why it's smart to commit to it. In the last few days of study, you'll discover what to do with all that knowledge.

Close today's study with a prayer, beginning,

Father, now that I know the truth, I want to. . . .

Now What?

You've seen the commercials.

A Super Bowl winning quarterback is running off the football field. He stops to grin at the camera. An off-camera voice calls him by name and asks, "You've just won the Super Bowl; what are you going to do now?"

A tennis pro serves the winning ace at Wimbledon and pumps her arms victoriously in the air. As she walks off the court, an off-camera voice calls her by name and says, "You've just won Wimbledon; what are you going to do now?"

The answer in each case, of course, is: "I'm going to Disney World!"

Suppose you're in a commercial right now. Two men approach you. One points a big black video camera at you, and the other shoves a microphone in your face. The man with the microphone calls you by name and says, "You've just learned Who decides what's right and what's wrong, how to recognize what's right, and how to consistently make right choices; what are you going to do now?"

What would you answer?

_____

_____

_____

The Next Step

Of course, you're not the first to make new and sometimes startling discoveries about truth. Others have done so before you. Why not look at what they did upon learning the truth. Perhaps their example is one you can follow.

Read the the following accounts of various individuals who encountered the truth. Complete the question following the name and the reference, and write how you think that person would have answered the question, "What are you going to do now?"

2 Chronicles 34:8,14-21,29-32— "Josiah, king of Judah, you've just_____

_____. What are you going to do now?"

_____

Daniel 5:1-6,10-17—"Daniel, you've just _____

_____. What are you going to do now?"

_____

_____

John 1:43-46—"Philip of Bethsaida, you've just _____

_____. What are you going to do now?"

_____

John 20:10-18—"Mary Magdalene, you've just _____

_____. What are you going to do now?"

_____

_____

What did each of those individuals do upon obtaining new insight into the truth?

_____

_____

To Tell the Truth

You see, if we learn how to make the right choices when we're faced with moral decisions, we possess a priceless knowledge. And that very knowledge carries a profound responsibility.

Think about it. Using what you know of the 4Cs process, what would be the right thing to do with that knowledge? Take a moment to:

Consider the choice. Remind yourself who decides right from wrong.

Compare it to God. Has He issued any precepts to guide you in this matter? If so, what are the principles behind those precepts that reflect the nature and character of the person of God Himself?

Commit to God's way. If a review of the precepts, principle, and person of God have made clear which is the right choice, commit to His way and do the right thing. . . with the help of His Holy Spirit.

Count on God's protection and provision. Whether or not the right choice promises immediate benefits, thank God for the loving motivation behind His precepts and wait in faith for Him to act in your best interests.

Have you concluded what the right thing to do with the knowledge of the truth is? If you're still uncertain, read _1 Timothy 2:3-4_. What does God want to happen?

_____

_____

The 4Cs

Because you know the truth, God's call to you is to *tell* the truth. Of course, that's not always easy. And, believe it or not, there is definitely a good way and a bad way to tell the truth. . . which is what we'll discuss in tomorrow's study.

Open your Bible to *1 Timothy 2:3-4* again. How do you react to those verses?

_____

_____

Respond honestly to the statements below, checking all that apply, to help you gauge how you're responding to today's study.

	Agree	Disagree	Don't Know
I don't want to tell others what I've discovered about the truth.	❏	❏	❏
I'm afraid to tell others what I've discovered about the truth.	❏	❏	❏
I don't think I have the right to tell others what I've discovered about the truth.	❏	❏	❏
I don't know how to tell others what I've discovered about the truth.	❏	❏	❏
I'd rather just know the truth myself and not feel like I have to tell others.	❏	❏	❏
I might be okay with telling others about the truth if I could find an easy nonthreatening way to do it.	❏	❏	❏

Take a moment to bow before God in prayer and discuss the responses with Him. Remember that your emotions and your will are not the same, so you may be honest about your feelings (the response of your emotions) while also committing to His way (the response of your will).

The Bold and the Beautiful

You sit down beside a group of your friends in the school cafeteria, staring uncertainly at the contents of your hot lunch. The school menu called it "Cheeseburger-something-or-other," but the only recognizable food item on your plate is the burger bun; everything else looks oddly out of place on a food tray.

You bow your head briefly over your tray, concentrating your thoughts on expressing thankfulness for something you're not sure is edible. Suddenly a hand grips your shoulder. You open your eyes and lift your head.

Mrs. Bronson is standing behind you. "Would you come with me?" she asks sweetly.

You glance uncertainly around the table at your friends, who look as puzzled as you feel. You leave your tray behind and follow the lunch room monitor into the hallway and into the school office. She leads the way into an empty office before turning around.

"What were you doing in there?" she asks.

You blink several times at her. "In where?" you ask.

"In the cafeteria. You were praying, weren't you?"

You blink faster. "Yeah," you say with a shrug. "Why? What's wrong?"

"You're on school property," she says.

You say nothing. You feel like someone who's tuned into a television mystery halfway through the show. *I've missed something important,* you tell yourself.

"I'm afraid I'm going to have to ask you not to do that," Mrs. Bronson says, firmly but sweetly.

"Not to do what?"

"Pray. You're not in church, sweetie, you're in school. Public school. With people of all different faiths. Some with no religious beliefs."

You say nothing. Your eyes narrow, as if looking for clues to the mystery you've entered.

"You may return to the cafeteria," Mrs. Bronson says, in a tone of dismissal.

You blink at her for a few moments before turning and walking, like a shell-shocked soldier, back to your lunch.

Get Real

Of course, that would never happen. Right?

Actually, it has happened. Cases very similar to the above have occurred in various schools, and even been tried in the courts.

People like Mrs. Bronson usually believe that they are promoting tolerance. They think that Christians who talk about the truth (about God, Christ, or right and wrong) or pray politely in a public place are displaying intolerance toward those who do not agree with them.

This concept of tolerance has arisen in our culture as a new cardinal virtue. It has become synonymous with goodness and open-mindedness; intolerance has come to connote bigotry.

Tolerance can be a good thing. Godly people will give due consideration to people whose practices differ from their own; they will be courteous and kind to those who don't view things the same way they do, refusing to judge anyone unkindly because God is the only One capable of judging righteously (*Ps. 9:3-10; Rom. 14:10-13*).

But the fact that we are not to pass judgment on each other does not change the fact that truth is absolute. It is God's job to judge; it is our job to live according to His truth, and to share that truth in love and compassion.

Daniel's Stand

So how do you do that? How do you "tell the truth" candidly and kindly? How do you balance absolute truth and appropriate tolerance?

Once again, you have a great example in Daniel, the Hebrew refugee who rose to prominence in Babylon.

Open your Bible to *Daniel 6* and read *verses 1-9*.

Verse 4 of the scriptural account mentions something about Daniel's character and behavior. What does it say?

Daniel balanced the truth and tolerance.

_____

_____

_____

_____

_____

Why is that so important for someone who is about to take a stand for truth?

_____

_____

_____

_____

_____

_____

_____

_____

Read *verses 10-16,* which describe how Daniel took a stand for truth. Place a check by the following words you think describe his behavior (check all that apply):

- ❏ obnoxious
- ❏ angry
- ❏ determined
- ❏ bitter
- ❏ disrespectful
- ❏ sarcastic
- ❏ haughty
- ❏ spiteful

- ❏ resolute
- ❏ quiet
- ❏ confident
- ❏ unkind
- ❏ polite
- ❏ wimpy
- ❏ brave
- ❏ embarrassed

A Daniel—like Stand

Judging from Daniel's example, what kind of attitude do you think you should take in standing for truth among those who do not share your beliefs or practices?

_____

_____

_____

What would it mean for you to follow Daniel's example in "telling the truth" to those around you?

_____

_____

What would you say to those who claimed that by taking a stand for truth you are not respecting their right to decide what's true for them?

_____

_____

_____

Close today's study by completing the following prayer in your own words:

Father, I know that you want everyone everywhere to "be saved and to come to a knowledge of the truth" (1 Tim. 2:4). Thank You for Your salvation and Your truth. Please help me to. . . .

A Den of Lions

day 4

You sit down beside a group of your friends in the school cafeteria, staring uncertainly at the contents of your hot lunch.

I gotta start brown-baggin' it, you decide. *This stuff can't be good for my insides.*

You bow your head over your tray to pray for your food (it needs it!). Suddenly you remember your little conference yesterday with Mrs. Bronson. You jerk your head up and open your eyes. Everyone around you is staring. . . at you. The news about what Mrs. Bronson told you has apparently gotten around school.

You freeze, gripping the sides of your tray with your hands. *It's just a short little grace. I've forgotten to pray lots of times before this.* You figure it's no big deal. You could even say a quick prayer with your eyes open and no one would know the difference. It sure would save a lot of trouble.

You realize your food is getting cold, and Tonya Sheldon's eyes look like they're going to roll out of her head if she stares at you any longer. *I sure don't want to be intolerant,* you think. *But I'm not standing on the table shouting a prayer at the top of my lungs; I just want to give thanks for my food*—you look at the food on your tray—*whatever it is.*

You look over your shoulder, and standing by the cafeteria door about 15 feet away is Mrs. Bronson. And she's watching you. Like a hawk.

What would you do? Based on what you have discovered about truth and tolerance, how would you resolve the above situation? Would you:

❏ Pray with your eyes open?
❏ Skip your prayer and ask God for forgiveness later?
❏ Close your eyes and pray longer than ever before?
❏ Do just as you had always done?
❏ Something else _____

What would you do? Would it be possible for you to take a stand for truth without being intolerant of others who don't share your beliefs or customs?

❏ Yes, because _____

_____

❏ No, because _____

_____

Can you obey the truth and still be tolerant?

Do you think it's intolerant of Mrs. Bronson to tell you not to pray in the school cafeteria?

❑ Yes, because _____

_____

❑ No, because _____

_____

A Night with the Lions

What did Daniel do in a similar situation? Turn to *Daniel 6* and read *verses 6-23.*

How did Daniel respond to the news that his beliefs and practices had been banned? *(v. 11)*

_____

Do you think his behavior was "intolerant" of the Babylonians' religions and customs?

❑ Yes, because _____

_____

❑ No, because _____

_____

Do you think Daniel knew that standing for truth might bring unpleasant consequences?

❑ Yes   ❑ No

How did Daniel treat the king after surviving a night with the lions *(vv. 21-22)?* Check all that apply:

❑ disrespectfully
❑ by praising God
❑ happily
❑ bitterly
❑ respectfully
❑ sarcastically
❑ spitefully

❑ angrily
❑ apologetically
❑ confidently
❑ unkindly
❑ politely
❑ haughtily
❑ with dignity

Compare *Daniel 6:16-17* to *Daniel 6:23-28.* What was the immediate effect of Daniel's stand for truth *(vv. 16-17)?* _____

_____

What was the eventual result *(vv. 23-28)?* _____

_____

Take a Daniel-like stand!

Your Stand for Truth

Using the items you checked on page 131 and 133 as a guide, what guidelines can you lay down to help you take a Daniel-like stand in a Babylonian-type culture? (For example, you may decide, "When I stand for truth, I will speak respectfully, act kindly. . . etc.") Write your guidelines below:

_____

_____

_____

_____

_____

Do you think that kind of behavior will guarantee that you'll never be criticized or accused of being intolerant?

❏ Yes, because _____

❏ No, because _____

If you were to adhere to those guidelines in the cafeteria situation with Mrs. Bronson, how do you think the story would end? Write your own ending for the story below:

_____

_____

_____

_____

_____

_____

_____

_____

_____

_____

_____

_____

_____

Close today's study in prayer, using a prayer like the following:

> Dear Father, I praise You because You are the living God and You endure forever.
>
> Help me to be like Daniel, who "was trustworthy and neither corrupt nor negligent" (Dan. 6:4).
>
> Help me to be like Daniel, who stood for truth and trusted you to stand for him;
>
> Help me to be like Daniel, who was not ashamed to tell the truth about You and Your commands, even when it meant facing lions;
>
> Help me to be like Daniel,
>> who was not afraid to stand alone,
>> who was not afraid to stand for truth,
>> who was not afraid to stand on Your Word. Amen.

The Stand

"He won't let me hit it, Daddy!"

The new Little Leaguer had struck out. He ran to his father and protested tearfully about the pitcher's uncooperative conduct.

The father, although moved by his son's tears, didn't complain to the umpire or scream at the opposing pitcher. He gripped his son's shoulders and faced him squarely.

"He's not supposed to let you you hit it, son," the man explained. "His job is to pitch the ball. Your job is to hit it. That's baseball."

Because we live in a Babylonian-type culture, we often feel like that woeful Little Leaguer. Evil seems to oppress us on every hand. The media, the public schools, the government, often seem hostile to Christians. Our beliefs are constantly questioned; our values are constantly assaulted.

It doesn't seem fair sometimes. But it should not surprise us that the truth is so often under attack. In a world in which we struggle *against the powers of this dark world and against the spiritual forces of evil in the heavenly realms (Eph. 6:12),* we should not expect the truth to be unopposed. We should, however, be prepared to stand for the truth when it is ignored or attacked. And we must do that with every weapon at our disposal.

The Weapons of Our Warfare

Read *Ephesians 6:10-18.* As you read, list the armor and weapons Paul mentions:

the belt of _____

the breastplate of _____

the readiness that comes from _____

the shield of _____

the helmet of _____

the sword of _____

Keeping in mind the story of Daniel (from the past two days of study), answer the following questions, checking all answers that you think apply:

1. Having "the belt of truth" buckled around my waist might mean:
❑ buying a belt buckle engraved with Scripture verses
❑ applying the 4Cs to my decision-making

❑ standing for truth when it is ignored or challenged
❑ recognizing God as the One who decides right from wrong
❑ other _____

2. Having "the breastplate of righteousness in place" might mean:
❑ making sure my living reinforces (not contradicts) my speaking
❑ having a hard time buying clothes that fit
❑ committing to God day-by-day and moment-by-moment
❑ other _____

3. Having my "feet fitted with the readiness that comes from the gospel of peace" might mean:
❑ always being ready to explain what I believe (and how it helps me) to others
❑ politely defending the truth about God, Christ, and right and wrong
❑ no more shoes from K—Mart
❑ other _____

4. Taking up "the shield of faith" might mean:
❑ never admitting that I have any doubts
❑ switching to a new deodorant
❑ trusting in God's protection and provision even when I don't see the benefits
❑ other _____

5. Taking the "helmet of salvation and the sword of the Spirit, which is the word of God" might mean:
❑ referring decisions about right and wrong to God and His Word
❑ devoting myself to daily prayer and Bible study
❑ a guest spot on "American Gladiators"
❑ other _____

The Full Armor

Therefore, Paul wrote, *put on the full armor of God, so that when the day of evil comes, you may be able to stand your ground, and after you have done everything, to stand (v. 13).*

Stand for truth, then, unashamedly telling your family, friends, and acquaintances the truth about right and wrong, about how to make right choices, and about the loving God who longs to protect and provide for all of us.

How can you do that?

• Practice the 4Cs process for making right choices, relating this biblical process to the moral decisions you face.

• Encourage others to give thoughtful consideration to the choices they make (and the consequences that result).

Put on the full armor of God.

• Use television shows, songs, and news events as springboards for discussing the 4Cs with your friends who have been through the course with you. ("What would happen if we apply the 4Cs to that person's choice?")

• If your youth group has not already done so, encourage your friends and leader to begin reaching out to others using the *Setting Youth Free to Make Right Choices* Video Series.

• Suggest that your youth group begin the *Right Choices* Workbook and group sessions with a new group of youth, perhaps giving you and your friends an opportunity to lead others through the course.

Are You Ready?

Are you ready to make right choices? You can do so consistently by evaluating every decision according to the 4Cs:

Consider the choice
Compare it to God
Commit to God's ways
Count on God's protection and provision

With that powerful prescription, you can experience something worth sharing—the truth that sets you free. . . to make right choices.

The 4Cs

extras

Passing on the Truth to Our Next Generation

The "Right From Wrong" message, available in numerous formats, provides a blueprint for countering the culture and rebuilding the crumbling foundations of our families.

Read It and Embrace a New Way of Thinking

The Right From Wrong Book to Adults

Right From Wrong - What You Need to Know to Help Youth Make Right Choices
by Josh McDowell & Bob Hostetler

Our youth no longer live in a culture that teaches an objective standard of right and wrong. Truth has become a matter of taste. Morality has been replaced by individual preference. And today's youth have been affected. Fifty-seven percent (57%) of our churched youth cannot state that an objective standard of right and wrong even exists!

As the centerpiece of the "Right From Wrong" Campaign, this life-changing book provides you with a biblical, yet practical, blueprint for passing on core Christian values to the next generation.

Right From Wrong, Trade Paper Book
ISBN 0-8499-3604-7

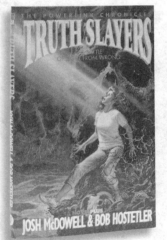

The Truth Slayers Book to Youth

The Truth Slayers - The Battle of Right From Wrong
by Josh McDowell & Bob Hostetler

This book—directed to youth—is written in the popular NovelPlus format and combines the fascinating story of Brittney Marsh, Philip Milford and Jason Withers and the consequences of their wrong choices with Josh McDowell's insights for young adults in sections called "The Inside Story."

The Truth Slayers conveys the critical "Right From Wrong" message that challenges you to rely on God's word as the absolute standard of truth in making right choices.

The Truth Slayers, Trade Paper Book
ISBN 0-8499-3662-4

Hear It and Adopt a New Way of Teaching

Right From Wrong Audio for Adults
by Josh McDowell

What is truth? In three powerful and persuasive talks based on the book *Right From Wrong*, Josh McDowell provides you, your family, and the church with a sound, thorough, biblical, and workable method to clearly understand and defend the truth. Josh explains how to identify absolutes and shows you how to teach youth to determine what is absolutely right from wrong.

Right From Wrong, Audio—104 min.
ISBN 0-8499-6195-5

See It and Commit to a New Way of Living

Truth Matters, Adult Video Series
ISBN 0-8499-8587-0

Video Series to Adults

Truth Matters for You and Tomorrow's Generation
Five-part Video Series featuring Josh McDowell

Josh McDowell is at his best in this hard-hitting series that goes beyond surface answers and quick fixes to tackle the real crisis of truth. You will discover the reason for this crisis, and more importantly, how to get you and your family back on track. This series is directed to the entire adult community and is excellent for building momentum in your church to address the loss of values within the family.

This series includes five video sessions, a comprehensive Leader's Guide including samplers from the five "Right From Wrong" Workbooks, the *Right From Wrong* book, the *Truth Slayers* book, and a 12-minute promotional video tape to motivate adults to go through the series.

Video Series to Youth

Setting You Free to Make Right Choices
Five-part Video Series featuring Josh McDowell

Through captivating video illustrations, dynamic teaching sessions, and creative group interaction, this series presents students with convincing evidence that right moral choices must be based on a standard outside of themselves. This powerful course equips your students with the understanding of what is right from what is wrong.

The series includes five video sessions, Leader's Guide with reproducible handout including samplers from the five "Right From Wrong" Workbooks, and the *Truth Slayers* book.

Setting You Free to Make
Right Choices, Youth Video Series
ISBN 0-8499-8585-4

Practice It and Make Living the Truth a Habit

Workbook for Adults

Truth Matters for You and Tomorrow's Generation
Workbook by Josh McDowell with Leader's Guide

The "Truth Matters" Workbook includes 35 daily activities that help you to instill within your children and youth such biblical values as honesty, love, and sexual purity. By taking just 25 - 30 minutes each day, you will discover a fresh and effective way to teach your family how to make right choices—even in tough situations.

The "Truth Matters" Workbook is designed to be used in eight adult group sessions that encourage interaction and support building. The five daily activities between each group meeting will help you and your family make right choices a habit.

Truth Matters, Member's Workbook ISBN 0-8054-9834-6
Truth Matters, Leader's Guide ISBN 0-8054-9833-8

Workbook for College Students

Out of the Moral Maze
by Josh McDowell with Leader's Instructions

Students entering college face a culture that has lost its belief in absolutes. In today's society, truth is a matter of taste; morality of individual preference. "Out of the Moral Maze" will provide any truth-seeking collegiate with a sound moral guidance system based on God and His Word as the determining factor for making right moral choices.

Out of the Moral Maze, Member's Workbook with
Leader's Instructions
ISBN 0-8054-9832-X

C A M P A I G N   RESOURCES

Workbook for Junior High and High School Students

Setting You Free to Make Right Choices
by Josh McDowell with Leader's Guide

With a Bible-based emphasis, this Workbook creatively and systematically teaches your students how to determine right from wrong in their everyday lives–specifically applying the decision-making process to moral questions about lying, cheating, getting even, and premarital sex.

Through eight youth group meetings followed each week with five daily exercises of 20-25 minutes per day, your teenagers will be challenged to develop a life-long habit of making right moral choices.

Setting You Free to Make Right Choices, Member's Workbook
ISBN 0-8054-9828-1
Setting You Free to Make Right Choices, Leader's Guide
ISBN 0-8054-9829-X

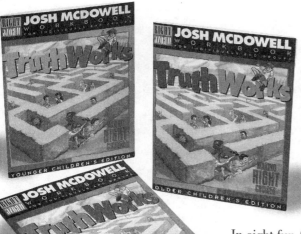

Workbook for Children

Truth Works - Making Right Choices
by Josh McDowell with Leader's Guide

To pass on the truth and reclaim a generation, we must teach God's truth when our children's minds and hearts are young and pliable. Creatively developed, "Truth Works" is two workbooks, one directed to younger children grades 1 - 3 and one to older children grades 4 - 6.

In eight fun-filled group sessions, your children will discover why such truths as honesty, justice, love, purity, self-control, mercy, and respect work to their best interests and how four simple steps will help them to make right moral choices an everyday habit.

Truth Works, Younger Children's Workbook ISBN 0-8054-9831-1
Truth Works, Older Children's Workbook ISBN 0-8054-9830-3
Truth Works, Leader's Guide ISBN 0-8054-9827-3

Contact your Christian supplier to help you obtain these "Right From Wrong" resources and begin to make it right in your home, your church, and your community.

Notes

SETTING YOU FREE TO MAKE RIGHT CHOICES